D1557098

PERSONAL FINANCE

ESSENTIALS

Saving and Investing

VOLUME IV

PERSONAL FINANCE

ESSENTIALS

Saving and Investing

VOLUME IV

JULIA A. HEATH

Facts On File
An Infobase Learning Company

Personal Finance Essentials: Savings and Investing
Copyright © 2012 Julia A. Heath

Facts On File, Inc.
An imprint of Infobase Learning
132 West 31st Street
New York NY 10001

Library of Congress Cataloging-in-Publication Data
Heath, Julia A.
  Personal finance essentials : saving and investing / Julia A. Heath
       v. cm
  Vol. 2 by Jane S. Lopus.
  Includes bibliographical references and index.
  Contents: v. 1. Decision making and budgeting—v. 2. Education and careers—v. 3. Credit and borrowing—v. 4. Saving and investing.
  ISBN 978-1-60413-986-0 (v. 1 : alk. paper)—ISBN 978-1-60413-987-7 (v. 2 : alk. paper)—ISBN 978-1-60413-988-4 (v. 3 : alk. paper)—ISBN 978-1-60413-989-1 (v. 4 : alk. paper)
1. Finance, Personal. I. Lopus, Jane S. II. Title.
  HG179.H374 2011
  332.024—dc22   2011004564

Facts On File books are available at special discounts when purchased in bulk quantities for businesses, associations, institutions, or sales promotions. Please call our Special Sales Department in New York at (212) 967-8800 or (800) 322-8755.

You can find Facts On File on the World Wide Web at http://www.infobaselearning.com

Text design by Erik Lindstrom
Composition by Erik Lindstrom
Cover printed by Yurchak Printing, Landisville, Pa..
Book printed and bound by Yurchak Printing, Landisville, Pa.
Date printed: February 2012
Printed in the United States of America

 Contents

Introduction   vii

1 Financial Institutions and Compound
   Interest   1

2 Risk and Return   27

3 The Bond Market   42

4 The Stock Market   63

5 Other Investment Options   96

   Test Your Knowledge   111

   Glossary   115

   Bibliography   125

   Index   127

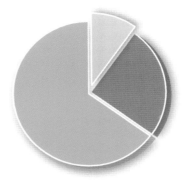

Introduction

What do you think of when you hear the term *financial literacy*? You probably have been hearing it a lot lately. As a result of the recent financial crisis, many people are calling for a greater level of financial literacy in the general population and among students in particular. But what does being "financially literate" mean? According to one popular notion, if someone knows how to write a check and balance his or her checkbook, then he or she is financially literate. Another view holds that someone who knows the benefits of saving is financially literate. These views all certainly reflect aspects of financial literacy, but they do not come close to describing what it really is.

In these volumes, we explore several topics: budgeting, getting an education, saving and investing, using credit wisely. Again, these are all components of what is commonly understood to be financial literacy. But also in these volumes is an emphasis on decision making—which is why it is the subject of the first volume in this series. The ability to make good decisions—identifying the important (and not-so-important) factors that should be considered, being able to weigh your options critically, being aware of the opportunity cost—is a skill that you will use over and over in your life. Being financially literate means that you understand how to make good decisions about money. So while the content of this set is an application of good decision-making skills, we hope that you recognize and apply the broader lessons to the nonfinancial aspects of your life as well.

When you hear the term *financial literacy*, do you feel excited to learn about it? Or anxious because you do not know anything about it, and you think it will be complicated? Or bored silly? Probably most people would choose the second or third answer—or maybe both. At the same time that there is general agreement that we need more financial literacy, it has gotten a bad rap. Financial literacy is often viewed as very complicated or, worse, extremely boring. It is neither. It just requires a change of perspective.

What if someone forced you to sit in a little box for several minutes each day—maybe for as long as an hour or more? You could not sleep, use your phone, or get up to walk around after a few minutes, you could not even let your mind wander. You would have to stay focused and just sit there. Does that seem like something you would be excited about doing? How excited were you when you learned to drive? When driving is described as it was above, it does not sound like something anyone would want to do. But you probably were very excited to learn to drive—not because of the physical movements associated with driving but because it represents independence and a rite of passage to adulthood. And it gets you from here to there.

The same is true with learning about financial literacy. Going through the mechanics of setting up a budget, a savings plan, investigating your education options, informing yourself so you do not fall victim to scams—none of that is very exciting in and of itself. But what it represents *is* exciting. It represents independence, being in control of your life. It represents a rite of passage—you are responsible for your financial future with the choices you make today. And it gets you from here to there. If you know or have talked to someone who does not have control over their financial lives, you have an idea of how consuming and debilitating the worry associated with that choice can be. The purpose of this set is to give you the skills you need to be purposeful in your decision making and to be able to take control of your life. Wherever your "here" is, with the help of these volumes, you can get to a better "there."

—Julia A. Heath and Jane S. Lopus

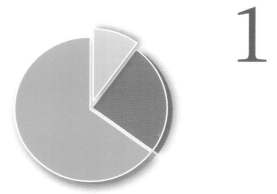

Financial Institutions and Compound Interest

Why do people save? After all, saving money is not nearly as much fun as spending it. Whenever someone saves money, he or she incurs an *opportunity cost*. The opportunity cost of saving money for the future is what could have been purchased today instead. So why do people save? When you cannot afford to buy something you want out of your current income, you must save money over time to buy it. At some point in your life, you have probably saved money to buy something that cost more than what you could afford in the current time period. People also save for college expenses, retirement, or for emergency funds.

In the first volume of this set, the idea of setting goals was introduced. In order to have an effective saving plan, it is very important to establish goals: what is it exactly that you are saving for, how much you can save each time period, and how long it will take you to reach your goal. Some goals can be achieved in a fairly short amount of time. For example, if you are saving to go to the prom or to buy your yearbook, you can usually achieve that goal in a few months. If you are saving to buy a car, or to help pay for college, the time period is longer. Finally, saving for a big purchase, like a house, or saving money for retirement are very long term goals. Unfortunately, the longer the time horizon for your goal, the more likely it is that you will have trouble staying with your plan for achieving it. The allure of instant gratification is always present, and sticking with your plan involves some discipline.

As you can see from the following graph, sometimes the country as a whole has had trouble choosing to save:

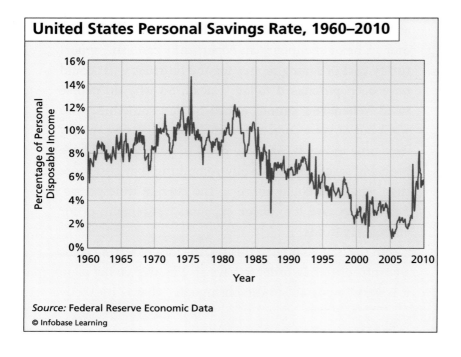

United States Personal Savings Rate, 1960–2010

Source: Federal Reserve Economic Data

© Infobase Learning

Since 1957, the personal savings rate has generally declined, hitting lows in 2005 and 2007. One of the consequences of individuals not saving is that they are more likely to engage in debt-financed spending, making their financial situation even more precarious.

Sticking with your plan is only one part of the challenge of saving. The other part of an effective savings plan is to know how to save wisely. There are many different ways you can save or invest, some of them risky. This volume will explore the ins and outs of saving and investing as a way for you to achieve your goals. After all, when you save and invest, you can not only reach your goals, but the size of your goals can actually increase. You could spend your money today on something small. Or you could save and invest your money, watch it grow, and achieve a much larger goal in the future.

Finally, a word about the term *investing*. When someone invests, they are spending resources now with the expectation that they will gain something in the future. In our context, we are referring to personal *investing*— spending or depositing money now to realize a future gain. There is also another type of investing, *capital investing*. Businesses and governments engage in capital investment, buying machinery, new buildings, and technologies to produce goods and services in the future. Again, our focus will be on personal investing.

COMPOUND INTEREST

"The most powerful force in the universe is compound interest."

Albert Einstein

Whatever your goals, the most powerful tool you have at your disposal to achieve them is *compound interest*. Very simply, earning compound interest is like snowballing your money. You start with an amount, you earn interest on that amount, then earn interest on that larger amount, and on and on. Your account gets bigger and bigger because interest is being paid on larger and larger amounts. To give a simple example, suppose you deposit $100 in a savings account that pays 10 percent interest annually. At the end of the first year, you will have $110 ($10 of interest plus the original $100). If you do not make any other deposits, at the end of the second year, you will have $121 ($11 of interest plus the $110 from year 1). At the end of year 3, you will have $133.10 ($12.10 in interest plus $121 from year 2). As you can see, once the original deposit is made, you are not only making money on that deposit, but on interest that your money has earned—other people's money! This is the power of compound interest.

Beginning of Year 1	$100
Beginning of Year 2 ($100 × .1) + 100	$110
Beginning of Year 3 ($110 × .1) + 110	$121
Beginning of Year 4 ($121 × .1) + 121	$133.10
Beginning of Year 5 (133.10 × .1) + 133.1	$146.43

Let us take a closer look at both how compound interest works and how it can help you achieve your goals. Assume we have two friends, Bert and Ernie. Both Bert and Ernie are the same age, have the same level of education, the same level of spending. The only thing that differentiates Bert and Ernie is their saving habits. Bert starts saving money as soon as he graduates from high school at age 18, saving $1,000 a year ($83.33 a month). But, Bert does not save for very long; in fact, he only saves for 11 years, until he is 28 years old, and then he stops.

On the other hand, his friend Ernie does not start saving when he graduates from high school. He waits until he is 29 years old to start saving, and then he saves at the same level as Bert—$1,000 per year. He continues saving throughout the years until he reaches age 65. Bert and Ernie's situations are summarized below:

BERT	ERNIE
Saves $1,000 per year for 11 years, from age 18 to age 28, then no additions thereafter	Saves nothing from age 18 to 28, then $1,000 per year for 37 years, from age 29 to age 65
Earns 7% interest per year	Earns 7% interest per year
How much more money will Ernie have at age 65 than Bert?	

While the details of the mathematical calculation may not be obvious, it is clear that Ernie has made the better saving choice, right? Wrong! Check out the table below to see what the results are of their savings plans.

AGE	BERT		ERNIE	
	Deposit	End-of-Year Balance	Deposit	End-of-Year Balance
18	$1,000	$1,070	$0	$0
19	$1,000	$2,215	$0	$0
20	$1,000	$3,440	$0	$0
21	$1,000	$4,751	$0	$0
22	$1,000	$6,154	$0	$0
23	$1,000	$7,655	$0	$0
24	$1,000	$9,261	$0	$0
25	$1,000	$10,979	$0	$0
26	$1,000	$12,818	$0	$0
27	$1,000	$14,785	$0	$0
28	$1,000	$16,890	$0	$0
29		$18,072	$1,000	$1,070
30		$19,337	$1,000	$2,215

Continued on page 6

AGE	BERT		ERNIE	
	Deposit	End-of-Year Balance	Deposit	End-of-Year Balance
31		$20,691	$1,000	$3,440
32		$22,139	$1,000	$4,751
33		$23,689	$1,000	$6,154
34		$25,347	$1,000	$7,655
35		$27,121	$1,000	$9,261
36		$29,019	$1,000	$10,979
37		$31,050	$1,000	$12,818
38		$33,224	$1,000	$14,785
39		$35,550	$1,000	$16,890
40		$38,039	$1,000	$19,142
41		$40,702	$1,000	$21,552
42		$43,551	$1,000	$24,131
43		$46,600	$1,000	$26,890
44		$49,862	$1,000	$29,842
45		$53,352	$1,000	$33,001
46		$57,087	$1,000	$36,381
47		$61,083	$1,000	$39,998
48		$65,359	$1,000	$43,868
49		$69,934	$1,000	$48,009
50		$74,829	$1,000	$52,440
51		$80,067	$1,000	$57,181
52		$85,672	$1,000	$62,254
53		$91,669	$1,000	$67,682
54		$98,086	$1,000	$73,490
55		$104,952	$1,000	$79,704
56		$112,299	$1,000	$86,353
57		$120,160	$1,000	$93,468
58		$128,571	$1,000	$101,081
59		$137,571	$1,000	$109,227
60		$147,201	$1,000	$117,943
61		$157,505	$1,000	$127,269
62		$168,530	$1,000	$137,248
63		$180,327	$1,000	$147,925
64		$192,950	$1,000	$159,350
65		**$206,457**	$1,000	**$171,575**

Adapted from *Financing Your Future*, Council for Economic Education, 2007

There are two things to notice here. First, Bert has accumulated almost $35,000 more by the time he reaches age 65 than Ernie has, even though he only saved for 11 years versus the 37 years that Ernie saved. Second, and more importantly, of the $206,457 that Bert has in his account, **only $11,000 of it is his own money**—$195,457 of his total amount is interest that has snowballed due to compound interest. Ernie, on the other hand, has deposited $37,000 of his own money, only earning $134,575 in interest.

As this example clearly shows, to meet your financial goals the most powerful tool you have in your possession is time, in the form of compound interest. Although Ernie contributed more than three times as much as Bert did, because Bert started so early, he was able to earn interest on interest. If Bert had continued to save throughout his working life until age 65, he would have accumulated about $378,000, only $48,000 of which would be his own money. Einstein was right!

There are compound interest formulas that will compute the future value of your account, but there are also many online tools that will do the calculations for you. You simply plug in a starting value (if you are just getting started, that value would be zero), how much you plan on adding each time period and for how long and what the interest rate is. These tools are very handy because they can motivate you to stick to your saving plan by keeping you focused on your goal. Some sites will tell you how much you need to be saving each time period to reach a certain goal, so you provide how much you want to end up with (for example, enough for a used car), and the rate of interest, and the program will tell you how much you need to save each time period.

These sites are very user-friendly and motivating, but there is an even easier way to get an idea of how quickly

Web sites for Computing Compound Interest!

http://www/moneychimp.com/calculator/compound interest calculator.htm

http://www.econedlink.org/interactives/interest.html

http://www.youngmoney.com/compound-interest-calculator.

There are many more—these are just a few of the most user-friendly ones.

your money will grow. This method is called the *Rule of 72* and will tell you how long it will take your money to double. To use the Rule, simply divide 72 by the interest rate you are earning and the quotient is the number of years it will take to double your money.

For example, if you deposit $1,000 in an account that is earning 8 percent interest and do not add any additional money to the account, you will have $2,000 in 9 years

Rule of 72

$$\frac{72}{\text{INTEREST RATE}} = \text{\# OF YEARS UNTIL MONEY DOUBLES}$$

($^{72}/_8 = 9$). If the account is earning 5 percent, it would take over 14 years for your money to double.

This brings us to the other important variable in achieving your financial goals: the interest rate. While time is on your side when you are saving for a goal, the interest rate you earn is also very important. As the example above shows, just a little difference in interest rates can mean a big difference in how long it will take to reach your goals. For example, in our Bert and Ernie example, if Bert had only been able to earn 5 percent on his account and had saved $1,000 per year for the entire period (48 years), he would only have accumulated $197,400 when he reached age 65, not the $378,000 he would have accumulated with a 7 percent return.

There is another factor that affects how much money you can accumulate, and some of the compound interest Web sites will ask you for this information. The final piece is the frequency of compounding, or the *compounding period*. If interest is compounded annually, that means that the interest earned on your account is only added to your balance once a year. On the other hand, if interest is compounded daily, it means that your earned interest is added to your account every day. In both cases, you are earning interest, but when it is compounded more frequently, you earn more because interest is added every day rather than once at the end of the year. If we go back and look at Bert, saving $1,000 a month for 48 years at 7 percent, if interest is compounded yearly, there is only one compounding period—interest is added only once in a year's time—and he accumulates $378,000, the amount we got earlier. If interest is compounded monthly—interest is added 12 times a year—he would accumulate $395,285, everything else the same. When interest is compounded weekly, his accumulation increases to $396,593 and if daily, it is $396,932.

To sum up, the two most important factors in determining whether you reach your financial goals are the interest rate you earn and the length of time the interest can accrue. Compound interest is a very powerful tool that can greatly enhance your wealth accumulation, particularly when you let time work for you. Remember Bert and Ernie—the vast majority of Bert's wealth was not his money; it came from his money snowballing through compound interest. The other, less important factor is how often interest is accrued.

Now that we have identified the critical components of building wealth, the next section will discuss the financial institutions that are available to you when you want to start saving your money.

FINANCIAL INSTITUTIONS

The first step in making sound and effective saving and investing decisions is to understand the financial institutions that form the basis for such decisions. We will examine several institutions in turn, but the best place to start is with the banking system.

The Banking System

The Federal Reserve. While most people have a fundamental understanding of how banks work, most do not fully understand how complex the banking system is and how their lives are affected by it. To get started, we need to take a brief step back in history, to 1913. The United States experienced two severe financial panics, once in 1893 and again in 1907. In an attempt to establish some stability in financial markets, the Federal Reserve Act was passed in 1913, creating the *Federal Reserve System*. The purpose of the Federal Reserve System was (and remains) to regulate the flow of money and credit in the economy to maintain steady economic growth.

The Federal Reserve System is a compromise between centralized and decentralized decision-making. The country is divided into 12 regions, each one containing a Federal Reserve Bank representing regional interests and perspectives. The Fed is governed by a *board of governors,* composed of representatives from seven of these regions and appointed by the President for 14-year terms.

If a bank is a *national bank* (that is, if it has many offices all across the country), the bank is required to be a member of the Federal Reserve System. State banks are able to be members of the System if they meet certain requirements. Most deposits held in commercial banks in the United States are held in member banks. The Fed acts as the bank for its member banks. Member banks borrow from the Fed, keep deposits at the Fed—all the things that individuals can do with their own banks. One of the tools that the Fed uses to maintain stable economic growth is to affect the interest rate that member banks can charge when they borrow money from each other. When this interest rate, called the *federal funds rate,* changes, the rate at which consumers can borrow money from their bank or the interest rate they can get on their time deposits will often change as well.

Interest Rates.   So, what does all this have to do with saving and investing decisions? Knowing what the current economic situation is and how the Fed might respond to it gives you good information about appropriate saving and investing options. For example, if it appears that the economy is slowing down, perhaps heading toward a recession, you might expect the Fed to lower the federal funds rate,

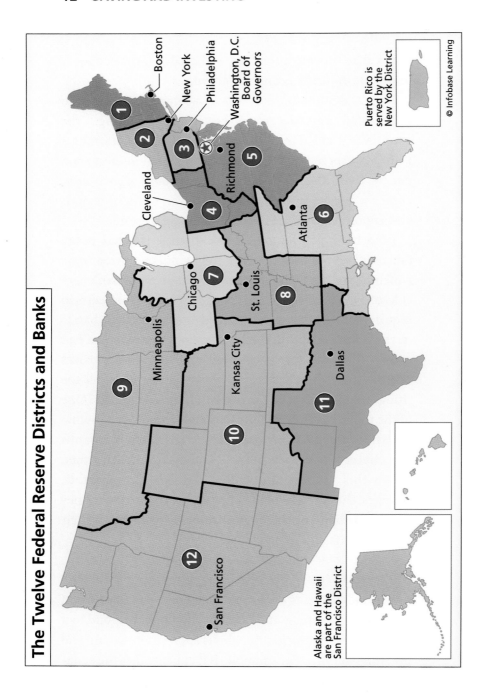

The Twelve Federal Reserve Districts and Banks

Boston
New York
Philadelphia
Washington, D.C.
Board of Governors
Cleveland
Richmond
Atlanta
Chicago
St. Louis
Minneapolis
Kansas City
Dallas
San Francisco

Puerto Rico is served by the New York District

Alaska and Hawaii are part of the San Francisco District

© Infobase Learning

making it easier for banks to lend funds to each other. Lowering the federal funds rate often results in decreases in consumer-related interest rates, so the interest rates on things such as savings accounts and certificates of deposit might fall. If you anticipate falling interest rates, you might want to lock in relatively higher interest rates with longer-term certificates of deposit before the Fed takes action or switch to some of the other saving/investing options discussed below. Conversely, if the economy is "overheated" (unemployment is very low, GDP is high), the Fed might raise interest rates to put the brakes on the economy so that inflation does not become a problem. In this case, waiting to lock in an interest rate might be the best strategy, as the Fed's action could get you a higher return. As we saw in the previous section, small changes in interest rate can mean a very large difference in how much money you can accumulate over time. Therefore, knowing a little bit about how interest rates are determined and whether they are headed up or down can mean the difference between earning a lot on your money versus earning less.

Regulations.   The federal government established an independent agency, the *Federal Deposit Insurance Corporation (FDIC)* to oversee the banking industry. The FDIC has responsibility for many aspects of the banking sector, but for consumers, the most important function is to provide insurance for depositors in case of bank failure. When a bank or savings association is a member of the FDIC, deposits are insured for up to $250,000 (per owner) for all deposit accounts held at a single bank, including checking, savings, money market, and certificates of deposit. Participating banks are required to display the FDIC sign prominently, enabling you to quickly determine if your money will be safe. It is important to know that since its establishment in 1933, no depositor has ever lost any money due to a bank failure when the funds were covered by the FDIC.

Other Financial Institutions

There are other financial institutions that deal with saving and investing, the most important of which are *credit unions*. Credit unions perform the same functions as banks. The difference is that credit unions are owned by their members, with the board of directors being directly elected by the membership in a democratic process. Similar to banks, deposits at credit unions are insured by the *National Credit Union Share Insurance Fund* at the same levels ($250,000) as provided by the FDIC to banks.

Another financial institution you may have heard of is a savings association, or a *savings and loan association*. Like credit unions, S&L's are often owned by their members. Unlike credit unions, the main function of S&L's is to use members' deposits to provide loans for the purchase of homes—mortgages. Like banks and credit unions, the savings deposits at S&L's are insured, in this case by the *Federal Savings and Loan Insurance Corporation (FSLIC)*.

Services Provided by Financial Institutions

While services provided vary by type of institution, the following is a list of services commonly offered to consumers:

- Checking and savings accounts
- Certificates of deposit
- Loans, including car, education, mortgage, and personal

- Credit cards
- Debit cards
- Safe deposit boxes
- Investment services
- Insurance
- ATM access
- Direct deposit
- Some banks have a currency exchange desk where you can get foreign currency in advance of a trip

While you can certainly invest your money in the bond market or the stock market (see chapters 3 and 4), or even an online bank, it is important that you establish an account at a bank or credit union close to you. While the return on your money may be higher elsewhere, a bank or credit union close to you provides you with two very important things: a checking account and instant access to your money through ATMs.

Choosing the Right Bank or Credit Union for You

There are a number of factors that you should take into consideration when choosing a financial institution. The first question you need to answer is: What kind of account(s) are you interested in? If you are only interested in opening a checking account, you will need to consider the following factors:

- Minimum balances. Does the bank or credit union require a minimum balance on a checking account? Sometimes a minimum balance is expressed as a minimum average daily balance. Your balance can be below the minimum, as long as your average balance for the month is greater than the minimum. Other institutions set an absolute minimum: your balance must stay above the balance for the entire month. In both cases, if you do not adhere to the minimum requirements, you will be assessed a fee.

- Check fees. Are you charged a fee for each check you write? Or for each check you write over a certain number?

- ATM fees. What are the fees for using your *ATM (automatic teller machine)* card? Are the fees charged only if you use your ATM card at other institutions' machines, or are the fees charged regardless of whether the ATM belongs to your bank or is owned by another bank? Does your bank charge for other transactions at the ATM, such as checking account balances?

- ATM locations. Are ATM locations convenient to your home? Your work? Since so much of financial transactions today take place at ATMs, you should be more concerned about the convenience of your bank or credit union's ATMs than where their branch offices are located.

- Overdraft charges. If you spend more money than you have in your checking account, either by writing a check or by using your ATM or debit card, you will be charged an *overdraft fee.* This bank fee can be as high as $30 for each bounced check, in addition to the bounced check fee the merchant assesses. Most banks now offer "overdraft protection" on checking accounts, but this can be very expensive protection. With overdraft protection, if you overdraw on your account, the bank can choose to allow the transaction and "cover" you for the difference. This service is not free. The bank can charge you $30 to $40 each time it covers you for the shortfall. In addition, this overdraft fee can actually increase each time you need to be covered.

For example, let us assume that you made a mistake in calculating your checking account balance, and you do not have as much in your account as you think you do. You have deposited a check and think you have sufficient funds in your account, but the check has not yet cleared, so the funds are not actually in your account yet. You do not realize that the check has not cleared, so you use your debit card to buy a magazine at the corner store, a cappuccino at the local coffee bar, and to buy a ticket to the movie that just came out. Each time you use your debit card, the bank charges you an additional overdraft fee, so you have just been assessed this $30 fee three times. And you still do not know that there is a problem.

New regulations require financial institutions to solicit your explicit permission for overdraft protection. If you "opt in," you will be covered when you overdraw your account, but you will be assessed the fees when you do. If you have a savings account at the same financial institution, the amount of your overdraft can be covered by transferring funds from savings to checking. There is usually no charge for this transfer. Some institutions limit how many times overdraft transfers can occur in one month.

Alternatively, you can choose to not opt-in. In this case, when you try to use your debit card and you have insufficient funds, the transaction will be denied. You will not be able to complete your purchase, but you will not be assessed any fees.

- Online account access. Most banks and credit unions offer online account access so you can keep track of your account (and help avoid the situation above). You can still get account statements mailed to you, but some banks will charge for this service.
- Cell phone access. More and more banks are adding the convenience of accessing your accounts via your cell phone. If this is a feature that is important to you, make sure there are no additional charges.

To summarize, if you are only interested in opening a checking account

- Ask for free checking with no minimum balance and no limit on the number of checks you can write. To get this service free you might have to sign up for direct deposit of your paycheck (a good idea anyway) and/ or ask about a "student" account, which often has these features. Checking accounts that pay interest may sound attractive, but some come with high minimum balances, so make sure you can maintain the balance or you will lose whatever interest you earn

A young woman withdraws money from an automatic teller machine (ATM). According to the Student Monitor annual financial services study, 72 percent of monthly college spending is with cash and debit cards. *(Shutterstock)*

on fees when your balance drops below the minimum.

- Ask about ATM fees, particularly the fees for using another institution's machine. Be aware that not only may your own bank charge you for using another machine, but the institution that owns that machine will also charge you. Therefore, if you think you will use an ATM frequently, having your own bank's machines close to where you work and live can save you a lot of money. Instead of using the ATM to withdraw cash, use the "cash back" option available at grocery stores, drugstores and many others. You get walking-around money, and you are not assessed any fees.

- Make sure you completely understand the overdraft protection plan. Ask if the bank offers alerts to tell you when you have a negative balance. If you are not completely comfortable with the plan, turn it down.

If you are concerned about going negative (infrequently), you can get overdraft protection without paying the fees with an overdraft line of credit. In this case, the bank covers the overage, just as before, but instead of charging you a fee, it treats the coverage as a loan. The interest rate on these loans can be fairly high, so make sure you understand the fine print. The best way to protect yourself against the infrequent overage is to also have a savings account at the same bank. Some banks will automatically transfer funds from your savings account to cover the shortage in your checking account, but some banks require that you request the transfer. Even if the service is automatic, sometimes there is a limit on how many automatic transfers are made in a month, so if you are out using your debit card, you could easily go over that number without knowing it. Once you exceed the number of transfers allowed, any additional overage is treated like a bounced check, and you are back to the worst case scenario that began this section.

If you are considering opening a checking account or want to reevaluate your current account, use this decision making grid to help you ask the right questions and make a decision about which institution is best for you:

ALTERNATIVES	CRITERIA				
	Free checking/no minimums	ATM fees/fees for other services?	ATM locations convenient?	Online banking?	Mobile banking?
Institution #1					
Institution #2					
Institution #3					
Institution #4					
Institution #5					

Once you've gathered and organized all the information above, you can decide which features of an account are the most important to you.

An additional option is to open an account with an online bank. (Note: this is different than conducting online banking with a bank that has an actual physical presence in your town. Online banks typically do not have any—or very few—physical banks or branches.) Because online banks do not have actual buildings to maintain, they can sometimes pay a higher rate of interest on various accounts, which might seem attractive. But, do your homework. One of the main concerns with online banks is their ATM network. If they do not have their own ATMs, you will be paying extra for the use of other institutions' machines. If they do have their own ATMs, how many are convenient to you? What are the fees? If they do not have ATMs that are convenient, and you do not have direct deposit, you will have to mail them your paychecks. If this is the case, how long does it take the

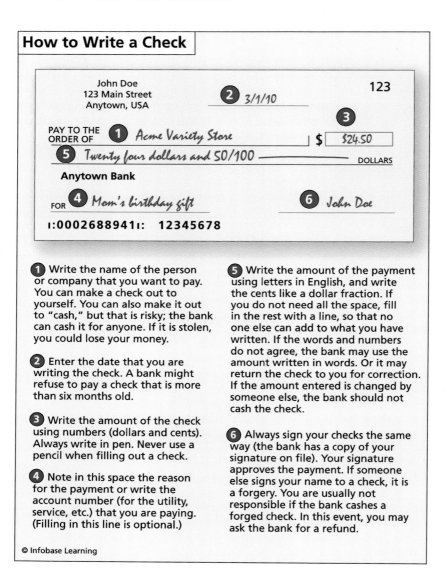

How to Write a Check

John Doe
123 Main Street
Anytown, USA

2 3/1/10

123

3

PAY TO THE
ORDER OF **1** Acme Variety Store | $ 24.50

5 Twenty four dollars and 50/100 ———————— DOLLARS

Anytown Bank

FOR **4** Mom's birthday gift

6 John Doe

⑆0002688941⑆ 12345678

1 Write the name of the person or company that you want to pay. You can make a check out to yourself. You can also make it out to "cash," but that is risky; the bank can cash it for anyone. If it is stolen, you could lose your money.

2 Enter the date that you are writing the check. A bank might refuse to pay a check that is more than six months old.

3 Write the amount of the check using numbers (dollars and cents). Always write in pen. Never use a pencil when filling out a check.

4 Note in this space the reason for the payment or write the account number (for the utility, service, etc.) that you are paying. (Filling in this line is optional.)

5 Write the amount of the payment using letters in English, and write the cents like a dollar fraction. If you do not need all the space, fill in the rest with a line, so that no one else can add to what you have written. If the words and numbers do not agree, the bank may use the amount written in words. Or it may return the check to you for correction. If the amount entered is changed by someone else, the bank should not cash the check.

6 Always sign your checks the same way (the bank has a copy of your signature on file). Your signature approves the payment. If someone else signs your name to a check, it is a forgery. You are usually not responsible if the bank cashes a forged check. In this event, you may ask the bank for a refund.

© Infobase Learning

check to clear? Sometimes it is difficult if not impossible to talk to a real person. Does that matter to you?

Regardless of the type of financial institution you choose, once you open a checking account you will need to reconcile your checkbook periodically—once a month should be fine. This is important to make sure your bank

How To Balance Your Checkbook

1. In your register, check off everything that both you and the bank have recorded (cleared checks, debit card purchases, deposits—everything)
2. In your register, add interest that your bank has credited to your account and subtract any fees that your bank has debited your account. This new balance is what you will compare in Step 7, below.
3. In the columns below, list deposits that you have recorded in your register but that do not appear on your bank statement. Also list debits that you have recorded in your register, but that do not appear on your bank statement.

Outstanding Deposits (Credits) That Do Not Appear on Your Bank Statement		Outstanding Checks, Debit Purchases (Debits) That Do Not Appear on Your Bank Statement	
Date	Amount	Date	Amount
Total		Total	

4. Enter the ending balance from your bank statement $_____
5. Add outstanding deposit total from above   + $_____
6. Subtract outstanding checks, etc. from above   – $_____
7. New balance (should match the balance in your checkbook register (after you have added interest and subtracted fees)   = $_____

has not made a mistake (it happens), and to make sure you have not forgotten to record something. If you start writing checks or using your debit card when you have insufficient funds, you will be charged with fees.

So, once a month, set aside 10 minutes or so to make sure you and your bank are on the same page. First, with your checkbook register and the bank statement (or electronic record) in front of you, check off those checks, ATM withdrawals, and/or debit card purchases in your register that have cleared your bank. Second, in your register, check off the deposits that have cleared your bank. Third, in your checkbook, record any interest and/or fees that your bank has credited or debited. Fourth, list any deposits that you have made that are *not* shown in your bank statement. Also list any outstanding checks, ATM withdrawals, and/or debit card purchases that do *not* appear on your bank statement. Finally, starting with the balance in your bank statement, add to it the deposits that do not appear on your bank statement, subtract from it the checks and other debits that have not cleared, and get a new balance. This new balance should be the same as the balance that appears in your checkbook register.

So far we have focused on checking accounts. But let us assume that you took the Bert and Ernie example to heart and have decided that you should start saving some money, too. Banks and credit unions offer a few options for you, but they are not terribly attractive in terms of return. A typical *passbook savings account* usually has a low minimum deposit and is easy to access. When linked to your checking account, it can provide overdraft protection minus the fees, as discussed above. Unfortunately, savings accounts pay notoriously low rates of interest, often not even paying enough to keep up with inflation (more about this is in the next chapter).

A step above a savings account is a *money market account*. These accounts are just as easy to access in case you need your money in a hurry and tend to pay a little bit higher interest rate (internet banks pay higher still), but the interest rate is still fairly low. The further disadvantage of money market accounts is that they generally have higher minimum deposit requirements (sometimes $1,000 or more). Banks and credit unions also offer CDs—*certificates of deposit*. CDs are savings "instruments" that you purchase that pay you a set rate of interest for a certain period of time. CDs usually pay a higher rate of interest than savings accounts or money market accounts, but the tradeoff is that you cannot get your money easily—you are locked into a specific time period. If you need your money before the time period is up, you pay a very stiff penalty. CDs can be purchased for a wide variety of time periods, from three months to many years. CDs also have a minimum purchase amount, usually $1,000. When you buy a CD, it is for the amount you deposit—you do not make additional deposits to the original CD, although you can purchase another CD.

Remember the section above on the Federal Reserve system where interest rate determination was discussed? Here is where a little knowledge about how that process works comes in handy. Assume that the economy has been humming along at a fairly good clip—GDP is strong, unemployment is low. If you were considering buying a CD, you might want to wait a bit. If the economy is heating up, the Fed might consider raising interest rates to "cool" it off a little so inflation does not get too high. Raising the federal funds rate often results in consumer interest rates going up, so you might lock in a higher interest rate if you wait to see what the Fed will do. Conversely, if there are signs that the economy might be slowing down—new housing starts are down, factory orders are down—you might want to lock in an interest rate now. When the economy slows down enough, the Fed often lowers the interest rate in an effort to jump-start the economy. Knowing the signs to look for and anticipating what the Fed might do in response is helpful when considering locking your money into an instrument like a CD.

Summary

While saving money does not guarantee that you will meet all your financial goals, if you do not save, you most certainly will not reach them. Compound interest is the rocket that gets you from here to there, a rocket that picks up speed as you go. The interest rate, time and to a lesser extent, the compounding period are the fuel for the rocket. Banks and credit unions offer safe, insured ways to earn compound interest, as well as the convenience of checking accounts, ATMs, easy access to your money, and online banking.

The problem with relying only on financial institutions to meet your goals is that while your rocket is totally safe, it is not moving very fast. In the next chapter, this trade-off is explored in detail: How fast do you want to go versus how safe do you want the ride to be?

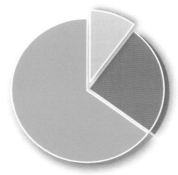

2

Risk and Return

In the last chapter, the concept of compound interest was introduced as the most important way to achieve your financial goals. We know that compound interest allows you to accumulate much more wealth than you could otherwise. However, we also know that how much wealth you accumulate is very dependent on what the interest rate is. If you rely solely on financial institutions such as banks or credit unions to increase your wealth, you might be waiting quite a long time. Banks and credit unions typically offer very low rates of interest on their savings and money market accounts, and even CDs. For some, this low rate is not worrisome because although their money is not growing very quickly, they know it is safe (as long as the financial institution is insured). For others, slow growth is not acceptable and will not allow them to reach their objectives. In this chapter, we will explore the relationship

27

between *return* and risk, and what that trade-off means for accumulating wealth. We will also examine the decision of how much risk to assume.

RETURN

The return on saving or investment is the *net* gain (or loss) that your savings/investing produces. For money that you put in a savings account, money market fund or certificate of deposit, this money will simply be the accrued interest. For example, if you deposit $1,000 in a two-year certificate of deposit paying 5 percent per year, at the end of the two years, you would earn a return of $102.50 (assuming annual compounding)—the interest earned. The calculation for this is straightforward:

$$\frac{Ending\ Balance - Beginning\ Balance)}{(Beginning\ Balance)} = Return$$

In our example this would be:

1102.50 – 1000 / 1000 = 0.1025 or 10.25%

But, the interest rate on the CD was 5 percent. Why is the computed return 10.25 percent? There are two answers to this question. The first is that the term of the CD was two years, so this 10.25 percent return is a two-year return. If we divide by two, we get an annual return of 5.125 percent—still not the same as our original 5 percent, bringing us to our second answer. The annual return of 5.125 percent is what is called an *annual percentage yield*, or APY. The APY simply reflects the additive effects of compounding. So, you earned 5 percent per year on your

Although 10–28 million people in the United States choose not to open a bank account, a savings account with a banking institution can earn interest, ensure against loss, establish good credit, and avoid check-cashing fees. *(Shutterstock)*

original $1,000, and the effects of compounding makes the return you actually receive 5.125 percent per year.

As we saw above, when your money is in a savings or money market account, or a certificate of deposit, the return is straightforward. When you have invested in another instrument, like stocks, bonds, or real estate, the calculation is a little more complicated. We will postpone a detailed explanation of the returns to stocks and bonds until later chapters, but basically, when you invest in these types of instruments, you may receive payments (called dividends for stocks and coupon payments for bonds), but the value of the investment itself can also change. For example, suppose you bought $1,000 in stock, paying an annual dividend of $50. The yield for this investment is 5 percent. But let us further suppose that by the end of the year, the stock that you bought for $1,000 at the beginning of the year is now worth $1,100. In other words, the price of the stock you bought went up. You have realized what is called a *capital gain*—an increase in the value of your investment. To get the total return on your investment, you must also take into account this increase in investment value:

Dividend	$50
Increase in Value	$100
Total return	$150

In this example, at the beginning of year you started with $1,000; at the end of the year you have $1,150 ($50 in dividends, $100 in increase in stock value). Therefore, your total return is

$1150 – $1000 / $1000 = 0.15 or 15%

As you can see, the return on investment is much larger than the yield. This may not always be the case. If the value of your stock had decreased in value, to say $980, your situation would be much different. You would still earn your dividend of $50, but you would also have a decrease in value of –$20, so your total return (in dollar amount) would be $30, and your percentage return would be:

$$\$1030 - \$1000 / \$1000 = 0.03 \text{ or } 3\%$$

In fact, if the value of your investment falls enough, your total return can actually be negative.

To summarize, yield refers to the income that is generated by an asset. In the case of savings/mutual fund accounts or CDs, this is simply the interest that accrues. On the other hand, the return on an investment is a larger concept that includes yield, but adds to it the change in the value of the investment itself. In the case of a savings/mutual fund account or CD, there is no change in the value of the investment, so yield and return are the same thing. For other instruments, however, these two values can be very different. Yield will always be positive, but return is not, necessarily. So which one is better for measuring performance? Because return is more inclusive, it is the measure that is typically used when evaluating the performance of various assets.

RISK

If someone asked you parachute from an airplane, would you do it? Most people would not. What if someone offered you $100 to parachute from an airplane. Would you do it now? Would you do it if the offer were $1,000,000? This is a simple example of the trade-off between risk and return. Most people would consider jumping out of an airplane a fairly risky thing to do and would not do it if someone just asked them to. If you offer $100, some people would think that was enough to compensate them for taking on the risk of jumping. With a $1,000,000 offer, a lot more people would think that amount compensates them for taking the risk. In other words, you would not be willing to take on the risk unless you received compensation that you thought was fair for doing something so dangerous.

Saving and investing involve the same trade-off. You can put your money in a very safe instrument, and you will not get much in the way of return. On the other hand, the only way you would be willing to risk losing your money on a dangerous investment is if you thought you would get a high return. But the analogy goes even further. If you do not parachute from an airplane, would you then claim that you were safe from all danger? Of course not. You could get hit by a bus, you could fall down an elevator shaft, you could get eaten by a bear. In other words, avoiding one type of risk (jumping out of a plane) does not make you immune from other kinds of risk. Likewise, when people think of the risk associated with an investment, they usually think of the probability of losing the original investment. We have all heard stories about a company going bankrupt and investors being left with nothing. Loss of principal is one type of investment risk, but it is only one of several, and protecting yourself from this kind of risk does not mean you are safe from other saving and investment dangers.

There are four main types of risk:

1. *Risk of Loss of Principal.* This is the risk that most people are familiar with—the chance

that you will lose all or part of your original deposit or investment—it is just gone.

2. *Market Risk.* Market risk means that the value of your investment may decline due to fluctuations in one or more markets. For example, if you bought gold at $1,000 an ounce, and now it is only worth $950 an ounce, the reduction in value is due to supply and/or demand changes in the market for gold.

3. *Interest-rate Risk.* With some investments, changes in interest rates can reduce their value. For example, if you buy a 12-month CD at 4 percent, and in the next month the interest rate increases to 5 percent, you are harmed because you are locked in at a lower interest rate.

4. *Inflation Risk.* Inflation risk is overlooked by a lot of people when they are making saving and investing decisions. Inflation risk means that the purchasing power of your investment has fallen. In other words, the return you get on your investment is less than the rate of inflation. For example, assume that you get a 3 percent return on a particular investment. You may realize this is not a great return, but you are not too unhappy with it. Until your friend points out that the rate of inflation for the past year was 4 percent. This means that if you deposited $100 at the beginning of the year and received $103 at the end, you are not really $3 ahead because the price of everything went up 4 percent over the year. You lost 1 percent in purchasing power.

To make good decisions about saving and investing, it is very important to keep all of these types of risk in mind. Remember the parachuting example? You could play it safe and never jump from a plane, but it does not mean you are safe. You could play it safe with your money and only deposit it in safe instruments, such as insured savings or money market accounts, or CDs. But doing so does not mean you are investing "safely." It means that you have eliminated the risk of loss of principal. But in doing so, you have exposed yourself to inflation risk since these instruments usually pay a very low rate of return, and in the case of a CD, possibly interest rate risk as well. In fact, even if you do nothing but put your money in an old sock, you are exposing yourself to inflation risk. The bottom line: **There is risk associated with every saving and investment decision, even the decision to not save or invest at all.**

Saving and investment decisions, then, involve making a series of trade-offs. There is a trade-off *between* risk and return—the greater the risk, the higher the return. There is a trade-off *among* the different kinds of risk. Minimizing the risk of loss of principal means that you incur inflation rate risk, at least. To make things even more complicated, there is a third criterion that must be taken into consideration when making saving and investment decisions: *liquidity.* The liquidity of an investment refers to how easy it is to change the investment into cash. A savings account, for example, is very liquid and is actually included in the most common definition of money in the United States. A work of art, on the other hand, might be a very good investment, but it is difficult to turn into cash quickly. A buyer must be found, a price must be agreed upon, the exchange must be made—all of which take time, making the art an illiquid investment.

The trade-off between risk and return can be presented as follows:

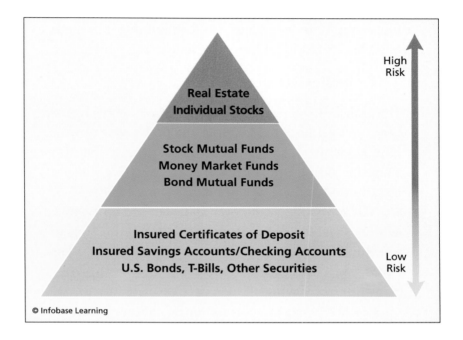

High
Risk

Real Estate
Individual Stocks

Stock Mutual Funds
Money Market Funds
Bond Mutual Funds

Insured Certificates of Deposit
Insured Savings Accounts/Checking Accounts
U.S. Bonds, T-Bills, Other Securities

Low
Risk

© Infobase Learning

RISK / REWARD PYRAMID

The risk referred to here is risk of loss of principal. While the base of the pyramid represents "safe" investments, this means relatively safe from loss of principal, not from such things as inflation risk.

Risk Tolerance

Now that you understand about the relationship between risk and return, let us more closely examine individuals' risk tolerance. As we will see, not only does risk have the components listed above (market, inflation, etc.), but it also comes from a couple of different sources. To talk about risk tolerance, we need to briefly discuss what is meant by expected return.

Briefly, *expected return* is simply the sum of each possible outcome, multiplied (or weighted) by the probability that the outcome will occur. For example, let us say you flip a coin. If it lands heads, you win nothing. If it lands tails, you win $10. The expected value of this situation is:

E = .5($0) + .5($10) = $5

The probability of getting a head is ½ or 0.5. If you get a head, you get nothing. Likewise the probability of winning $10 is also ½ or 0.5. Let us be clear about what this $5 means. Obviously, when you flip a coin once, you are not going to win $5. You are either going to win $0 or $10. But, if you flip a coin over and over, add up all your winnings and divide by the number of times you flipped, you would probably get something close to $5. In other words, you would expect to *average* $5 in winnings over many times of playing.

Now let us expand this notion of expected value to include risk. Let us say you are faced with two situations, each one giving you a choice:

 ## Situation 1

Choice A: You will be paid $10.
Choice B: You will flip a coin and be paid $30 if it is heads, $0 if tails.

Situation 2

Choice A: You will be paid $15,000.
Choice B: You roll a die and will be paid $5,000 times the number that you roll.

In Situation 1, would you choose A or B? What about in Situation 2? Let us look at the possible outcomes and the probabilities of each outcome; that is, the expected returns:

SITUATION 1				
	Potential Return	Probability	Expected Return	
Choice A	$10	100%	$10	
Choice B				Total
Heads	$30	50%	$15	
Tails	$0	50%	$0	$15
SITUATION 2				
	Potential Return	Probability	Expected Return	
Choice A	$15,000	100%	$15,000	
Choice B				Total
Roll a 1	$5,000	16.7%	$835	
Roll a 2	$10,000	16.7%	$1,670	
Roll a 3	$15,000	16.7%	$2,505	
Roll a 4	$20,000	16.7%	$3,340	
Roll a 5	$25,000	16.7%	$4,175	
Roll a 6	$30,000	16.7%	$5,010	$17,535

In both Situation 1 and Situation 2, your expected return is lower if you choose the safe route, Choice A. In both situations, choice A occurs with 100 percent probability—it is a sure thing—but the expected return is lower. You get a higher return if you are willing to take a risk. So we again see the trade-off between risk and return.

But this example gives us two additional insights into the risk/return relationship. If you chose Choice B in the first situation, did you also pick Choice B in Situation 2? Some people might pick the riskier option in the first situation, but decide to play it safe in the second situation. Why? First of all, the amounts of money in the situations differ greatly. In Situation 1, if you choose B and lose, you have lost what you would have received under Choice A, the sure thing. In other words, your opportunity cost of taking the risk is $10. In the second situation, your opportunity cost of taking the risk is much higher, possibly as much as $10,000 ($15,000 – $5,000—the smallest return under Choice B). Risking $10,000 is a very different animal than risking $10. Therefore, one of the factors associated with how much risk you are willing to take on (your *risk aversion*) is your relative wealth. To some, risking $10,000 would be nothing; to others, it would be a very big sum. The larger the amount risked, relative to your overall wealth, the less risk you will be willing to take on.

The second reason many people might take the risk in Situation 1, but play it safe in Situation 2 is that the variability of possible outcomes is much larger in the second case than in the first. If you take Choice B in the first case, your possible outcomes range from $0 to $30. In the second situation, your outcomes could range from a low of $5,000 to a high of $30,000, a much greater dispersion. Thus, the greater the dispersion of outcomes, the greater the risk of an investment. In fact, the degree of "spread" of an investment (called its *beta*) can be quantified and is the primary measure of its risk.

As we have seen, risk has many facets. Your willingness to take on risk, your level of risk tolerance, to some extent is a part of your psychological makeup. However, risk tolerance does not only vary *between* individuals; it also varies over time for the same individual. As discussed above, your willingness to take on risk varies according to your level of wealth. In addition, it also varies according to your time horizon relative to your goals. If you are saving/investing in order to meet a short-term goal, such as saving for a used car, you will be less tolerant of risk because there is less time to recover if your saving/investment instrument loses value. On the other hand, if you are saving/investing to meet a long-term goal, such as a down payment for a house or retirement, you have more time to make up any losses, so you would be willing to put your money in instruments that carry more risk.

Are you doomed to earn small returns because your time horizon is fairly short and you are relatively risk intolerant? Not necessarily. There are ways to manage risk, one of which is based on an old adage that you have probably heard: Do not put all your eggs into one basket. One way to manage risk is to spread your saving/investing dollars over different assets—diversify. When you practice *diversification* you may protect yourself against risk because if some of your assets fall in value, you have others that may increase in value. For example, if you take all your money, buy one stock, and the value of that stock decreases, your wealth has taken a big hit. On the other hand, if you take the same amount of money and buy several stocks, when one or two fall in value, your wealth still decreases, but the remaining stocks act as a buffer, protecting you from the full impact. Taking diversification further, if you own several different kinds of assets (stocks, bonds, CDs) you are protected to an even greater extent.

We can see the effect of diversification between as few as two stocks:

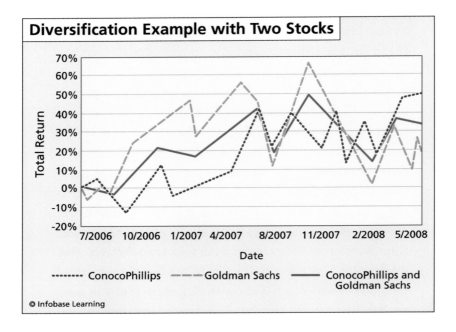

Diversification Example with Two Stocks

© Infobase Learning

The purple line represents the return to stock in Conoco Phillips, the orange line represents the return to stock in Goldman Sachs, and the green line represents the return to a portfolio that is composed of 50 percent of each stock. The volatility of the two stocks taken individually is significantly reduced when they are combined into a diversified portfolio. Adding even more stocks to this portfolio would further stabilize the return.

The other major way to manage risk is called *dollar cost averaging.* Dollar cost averaging is simply the process of investing a fixed amount at regular intervals. Thus, instead of trying to guess when stock or bond prices are low and buying then, you ignore the fluctuations of these prices and buy at the same time every week or month. The ups and downs of the markets (the risk) are "smoothed out" over the long run.

SUMMARY

When it comes to saving or investing your money, every option that you have available to you has its own risk. In general, the greater the risk you are willing to assume, the greater the return. But, there is more than one kind of risk, so each investment decision must be weighed in terms of both potential return and type of risk associated with it. In fact, saving your money by putting it in your piggy bank also has a risk associated with it. The key to making good investment decisions is to recognize the types of risk, think about your risk tolerance and your time horizon, and strike a balance that allows your money to grow, but also lets you sleep at night.

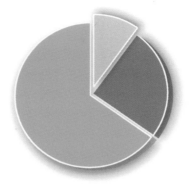

The Bond Market

You may be a participant in the bond market already—some of you from birth. Savings bonds are a common gift to bestow upon new parents, jump-starting a college fund or a general savings plan. Savings bonds are just one form of bond that is available, along with other government and corporate bonds. The bond market is similar in some ways to the stock market, although they represent a very different kind of asset.

WHAT IS A BOND?

Imagine that you and a friend are standing in line at the movie theater, waiting to buy a ticket. You suddenly realize that you left your money at home. You ask your friend to loan you the money for the ticket and promise to pay her back by buying her ticket the next time you go to the movies. In fact, you tell her that you will buy her popcorn at the next movie, too. She agrees, you both enjoy the movie, you buy her ticket and popcorn the next time. Believe it or not, this is very similar to how the bond market works.

A *bond* is an IOU. When you buy a bond of any kind, you are lending money to the entity that issues the bond, the borrower. There are many entities that need money to conduct their operations: the federal government, state and local governments, and corporations. One of the ways that these entities can get the money they need to operate is by borrowing money, and one way to borrow money is to issue bonds to the public.

When you buy a bond, the price you pay for the bond is called its *face value* or *par value*. This is the amount that the borrower promises to pay back at the end of term, or at the bond's *maturity date*. Just as you offered your friend an incentive to loan you money for the movies (buying her popcorn the next time), governments and corporations must offer an incentive to the public to loan them money. While the bond is maturing, some bonds pay interest during the term, called *coupon payments*. Coupon payments are typically made semi-annually and reflect the interest rate at which the bond was purchased. Other bonds, called *zero coupon bonds,* do not include a commitment to pay interest throughout the term. Instead, the price of zero coupon bonds is discounted (they are also called *discount bonds*), so the interest you earn on your investment is reflected in the difference between the discounted price you paid for the bond and the face value of the bond. Savings bonds issued by the government are examples of zero coupon bonds. The price of a savings bond is 50 percent of the face value. Once you have purchased it, the government does not send you periodic interest checks. Instead, you hold it until the maturity date (seven years) and cash it in for the full face value. So the earnings on your bond investment is the difference between what you paid and the face value.

The following schematic shows how coupon and zero coupon bonds work:

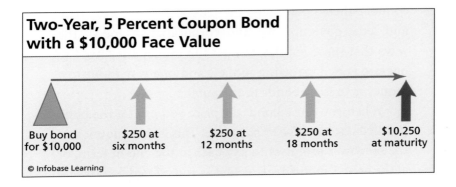

Two-Year, 5 Percent Coupon Bond with a $10,000 Face Value

| Buy bond for $10,000 | $250 at six months | $250 at 12 months | $250 at 18 months | $10,250 at maturity |

© Infobase Learning

This bond pays a 5 percent coupon payment every six months (5% × $10,000 = $500/2). It matures in two years, so at that time, you are paid the face value ($10,000) plus the final coupon payment of $250.

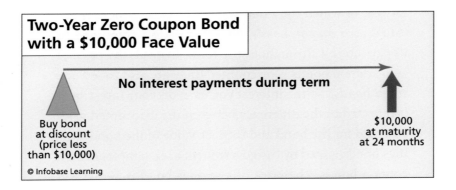

Two-Year Zero Coupon Bond with a $10,000 Face Value

No interest payments during term

Buy bond at discount (price less than $10,000)

$10,000 at maturity at 24 months

© Infobase Learning

Assume you buy this bond for $9,600. Since this is a zero coupon bond, no periodic payments are made. But, at the end of two years, you will be paid the face value ($10,000). Using the formula from the last chapter, this bond has a return of 4.2 percent ($400/$9,600).

Regardless of the type of bond (coupon or zero coupon) or the entity that issues the bond, all bond purchases involve a promise. The issuing entity promises to pay you the face value of the bond at maturity. The entity promises (in the case of coupon bonds) to make periodic interest payments to you. If you buy a bond and hold it to maturity, you know exactly how much money you will receive. As we will see in the next chapter, this is a much different environment than the stock market, where there are no promises. Bonds do carry risk, but because of the guarantees inherent in buying bonds, they are much less volatile than stocks. In fact, bonds are often called *fixed-income investments* due to the steady nature of their earnings.

HOW DOES THE BOND MARKET WORK?

When governments or corporations need to borrow money, they must somehow let it be known that they are willing to issue bonds. When investors are interested in buying the IOUs of these entities, they must be able to locate them, along with information on the borrower, the terms of the bond and the interest rate. In other words, like with other financial instruments, bonds are bought and sold in a market. When a corporation wants to finance its operations with debt and issue bonds, these bonds are initially sold to large investment banks. This initial sale of bonds to investment banks is where the funds are raised for the corporation. This is the *primary market*. Once the bonds have been purchased by investment banks and the issuing corporations have raised their funds, the bonds are then offered for sale by the investment banks to their customers. The buying and selling of bonds in this *secondary market* does not raise additional funds for the corporation—it is simply a transaction between the bank and another entity. In fact, after the first issuance of the bonds, the original issuing corporation is not involved in any future exchanges or the proceeds from the exchanges.

While many stocks are sold at physical locations, such as the New York Stock Exchange or the NASDAQ, most bonds are sold in what are called *over-the-counter markets*, OTCs. Over-the-counter markets simply refer to the brokers and others who operate in the secondary market for bonds.

HOW ARE BOND PRICES DETERMINED?

Assume that you have purchased the two-year, 5 percent coupon bond with a $10,000 face value that we illustrated above. As discussed, you pay $10,000 today for the bond. You will receive $250 every six months for the life of the bond (two years), with a final payment of the face value plus the last interest payment ($10,250). With a zero coupon bond, the amount you pay initially is not set in stone—the price is less than the face value ($10,000)—but is set by the market. It appears that in the first case, the price you pay for the bond is clear-cut—$10,000—while the price in the second case is open to market forces. Actually, the price of *both* bonds is open to market forces.

While some people buy a bond and hold it until it matures, many others sell bonds before their maturity dates, putting them on the secondary market where their prices are determined by demand and supply.

Let us go back to the zero coupon bond. You pay some discounted amount for it today, say $9,600, in return for a promise that you will be paid $10,000 in two years. Since it is a zero coupon bond, you do not get periodic interest payments: Your investment earnings come from the difference between the bond's purchase price and its face value. At the maturity date, you are paid $10,000, which is $400 more than you paid for bond two years ago. Therefore, you have earned about 4.2 percent on your initial investment. What if you had been able to purchase the bond for a lower price, for example, $7,500? At the maturity date, you would be paid the same $10,000, but this time you have earned $2,500 more than you paid for the bond or a 33.3 percent return ($2,500/$7,500). In this simple example, we see one of the fundamental relationships in the bond market. Bond prices and bond yields have an inverse, or negative relationship. In our example, when the bond price fell, the yield on the bond went up. To look at it from the other direction, if interest rates are increasing, what will happen to bond prices? If interest rates are increasing, that means you will earn more on your bond investment. The only way for you to earn more on your investment (that has a guaranteed, fixed face value at maturity), is if the initial price, the price you pay for the bond, falls.

The same relationship holds for coupon bonds as well. Our coupon bond example above is a two-year, 5 percent coupon bond with a face value of $10,000. You will receive payments of $250 every six months for the life of the bond. To compute the yield for coupon bonds, the computation is

Coupon / Purchase Price = Yield

For our example, that is $500/$10,000 or 5 percent, which is the stated coupon rate. This is called the *current yield.* When you buy a bond for the face value, the current yield is simply the coupon, or interest rate, in our case 5 percent.

What happens if you could buy this bond for less than $10,000? Let us assume you can buy this bond for $8,000. It will still pay $250 every six months for the term of the bond, two years, at which time you will receive $10,250. The yield on this bond is much higher than the coupon rate of 5 percent. Using our formula form above, we have $500/$8,000 for a yield of 6.25 percent. This is called the *yield to maturity.* Yield to maturity is the return of a bond for any given price. So, for a price of $10,000, our yield to maturity is 5 percent (the same as the current yield). But when the price decreases to $8,000, our yield to maturity increases to 6.25 percent. It is important to note here that the bond is still a 5 percent coupon bond since the coupon payments of $500 represent 5 percent of the face value of $10,000 (not the purchase price). The difference is in our initial purchase price of the bond. When we buy at face value, current yield and yield to maturity are the same thing. When we buy at another price (lower or higher), yield to maturity will be higher or lower than the current yield or coupon rate. In the world of bonds, *bond yield* is typically referring to yield to maturity. Again, notice that as the price of the bond fell (to $8,000), the yield increased (to 6.25 percent).

So which is better: high yields or high prices? It depends. If you are buying bonds, you want to buy at low prices (high yields). Once you own bonds, however, you want the prices to go up (yields to go down). Your yield is already locked in by the coupon payment, but if prices go up, you can sell your bond before the maturity date and make a profit.

BONDS AND RISK

We said earlier that bonds are also known as fixed-income investments because they pay a fixed amount at specified times with a guarantee of payment at maturity. You should not conclude from this that bonds are risk free. All bonds carry some amount of risk, but different bonds carry different kinds of risk. Although bonds provide a promise of payment, if the entity issuing the bond ceases to exist, all guarantees evaporate. A corporation could go out of business, for example, leaving you with a worthless bond certificate. Another type of risk is the risk of the bond being *called*. When a bond is called, the borrower pays it off early. You do not lose your money in this situation, as you do in the case of a default, but you do have to find another place to put your money. Not all bonds are callable, and the prospectus must tell you if it is and what the payout will be if it is called.

We will discuss the types of bonds in detail below, but for now, let us consider U.S. bonds. Bonds issued by the federal government are not callable, nor are they at risk of default. In fact, the interest rate on short-term bonds issued by the federal government is referred to as the *"risk free" interest rate*. Is it really? Remember that there are many kinds of risk with saving and investing, the loss of principal being only one. What risk do you think is involved in holding government bonds with a "risk free" interest rate? If you said inflation risk, you are correct. If you have purchased a long-term bond, you are locked in to an interest rate until the bond matures. Your return is in danger of not keeping pace with inflation over that period, particularly since "risk free" also means low return, as we have seen.

The other risk of long-term bonds is that the current market value of the bonds can decrease. Remember that in chapter 1 we talked about how some fundamental knowledge about the economy could be a significant advantage in making saving and investing decisions. This is another example of why that is so. If the economy is experiencing a lot of growth, that means unemployment is low, demand for goods and services is high, businesses are booming. The Federal Reserve, in an effort to keep inflation in check in a booming economy, might raise interest rates. As we know from the discussion above, when interest rates increase, bond prices fall—bad news for you if you currently own bonds and are thinking of selling them, but good news for you if you are considering buying them.

Figuring out the bond market can at times feel like you have fallen down Alice's rabbit hole. When the news is good, you feel bad as a bond holder, but good as a potential bond buyer. When the news is bad, you are elated as a bond holder, but not very happy as a bond buyer.

TYPES OF BONDS

Most bonds fall into one of four categories: bonds issued by the U.S. government; state and local bonds; corporate bonds; and mortgage-backed bonds. While the basic mechanics work the same for all of them, they vary widely in terms of risk and return.

U.S. Government Bonds

These bonds are risk-free because the face value is guaranteed by the government. Government bonds fall into three groups that only vary according to the time to maturity:

- *Treasury bills* (T-bills) have the shortest time to maturity and are available in three different lengths. T-bills with 91-day and 182-day maturities are auctioned off once a week by the Treasury. T-bills with 364-day maturities are auctioned off every four weeks. T-bills do not pay interest payments during the term and are sold at a discounted price that is determined by each auction.
- *Treasury notes* (T-notes) pay interest twice a year and are issued in maturities of two, three, five, and 10 years.
- *Treasury bonds* (T-bonds) also pay interest twice a year and are usually issued with a 30-year maturity.

The Treasury securities above are collectively called "Treasuries." All interest earned on U.S. government bonds is exempt from state and local taxes (but not federal).

These bonds are all sold at auction, which means that the price of the bonds varies. The interest rate is set for each bond, but as we discussed above, the interest rate is not the same thing as the bond's yield. If there is a large demand for bonds at any particular auction, the price of the bond will be bid up, selling at more than its face value. As a result, the yield on this bond will be low. You can think of it this way: Bond buyers had to pay more than the face value in order to get the bond's interest rate. On the other hand, if demand is low at any particular auction, the bond price will fall until buyers are willing to purchase the bond. If buyers can get a bond for less than the face value, the yield on that bond will be high.

The Treasury also sells savings bonds—EE bonds and I bonds. Paper EE bonds are sold at half their face value (so you can buy a $100 bond for $50, for example); electronic EE bonds are sold at full face value. The interest on EE bonds adjusts every six months and is tied to the interest rates of 10-year Treasury Notes. Interest is compounded semi-annually and added to the bond monthly. EE bonds must be held at least a year. After one year you can redeem your bond any time, but if a bond is held

EE bonds can be used to finance education and given as a gift. The interest on EE bonds adjusts every six months and is tied to the interest rates of 10-year Treasury notes. *(Shutterstock)*

less than five years, you must pay a three-month interest penalty. The Treasury guarantees that a EE bond will double its face value (or in the case of paper EE bonds, reach their face value) in 20 years. (Note—you know the Rule of 72, so what interest rate are they guaranteeing? Answer: 3.6 percent). The bonds will continue to pay interest for 30 years. Interest earned on the bonds is exempt from federal tax until the bond is cashed in and is forever exempt from state and local taxes.

The Treasury also issues a savings bond called an I bond—the I stands for inflation-adjusted. These bonds are sold at full face value. The return on an I bond is composed of a fixed interest rate (fixed for the life of the bond), plus an inflation adjustment factor that is recalculated every six months and is based on the Consumer Price Index. Like EE bonds, you must hold I bonds for at least one year and if cashed in before five years has passed, you must pay a three-month interest penalty.

Both the EE and I bonds are what we have learned are called zero coupon bonds; that is, bonds that do not make periodic interest payments over the life of the bond. Instead, interest is paid at maturity. While receiving periodic interest payments may seem attractive, one of the main advantages of zero coupon bonds is that many investors like instruments that have a definite maturity date. This, and the variety of denominations, is why savings bonds are popular with those who are saving for their child's (or grandchild's) college education.

State and Local Bonds

When state or local governments need to raise money for public projects, such as school construction, airports, parks, roads, and hospitals, they turn to "munies," *municipal bonds*. There are several different types of municipal bonds, and the differences between them involve how the borrower will repay the bonds.

General obligation bonds are similar to federal bonds in that repayment is guaranteed by the issuing entity, which can employ a variety of means to repay the obligation. Other bonds are specifically written to raise taxes or institute a new tax. Still other bonds are for revenue-generating projects, such as constructing a highway that will collect tolls.

Municipal bonds are generally considered very safe since they are backed by the government entity that issues them. There have been cases where government entities have been on the verge of bankruptcy, but by and large, these bonds have low risk of default. The interest earned on munies is exempt from federal taxes. State-issued munies are exempt from state and federal taxes, and local munies are exempt from taxes imposed by all three levels of government. So, if the risk is low and the proceeds are tax exempt, why does not everyone own munies? If you guessed the answer has something to do with the yield, you are correct. The yield on munies is usually low, both because the risk is low, but also because of the favorable tax treatment.

Corporate Bonds

When businesses need money to expand their operations, buy new machinery, or anything else, they can sell stock, they can borrow the money from the bank, or they can borrow from the public by issuing bonds. There are many different kinds of corporate bonds. Some bonds are "callable," meaning that the company can pay off the bond before the maturity date. Some bonds are *convertible*. Convertible bonds can be converted into shares of common stock under stated circumstances. The interest on corporate bonds can be fixed until maturity, or can be indexed (i.e., it changes) to Treasury bill rates. Some corporate bonds are offered as zero coupon bonds, with the same characteristics as discussed previously.

Corporate bonds are riskier than federal bonds or munies. If the business folds, you can lose your investment—they are not backed by "the full faith and credit" of anything other than the corporation, and there are no guarantees. The interest earned on corporate bonds is fully taxable. For both of these reasons, the yield on corporate bonds is typically higher than federal or muni bonds.

Mortgage-Backed Securities

When consumers take out loans to buy homes (mortgages), they may not know it, but they are creating an investment instrument. Many mortgages are bundled together, or "pooled" to create mortgage securities. These mortgage securities are offered for sale to investors, who then receive periodic payments that represent the interest and principal paid on the loan. Sometimes the entity that "pools" the mortgages and then offers them for sale is an agency of the government: the Government National Mortgage Association (Ginnie Mae), or an entity that is a quasi-government agency such as the Federal National Mortgage Association (Fannie Mae) or the Federal Home Loan Mortgage Corporation (Freddie Mac). Most of the mortgages that are bundled are done so by these agencies. Some private companies, such as investment banks and other financial institutions, also bundle mortgages.

You may have heard of *mortgage-backed securities* and the agencies discussed above. Mortgaged-backed securities played a very large role in the financial meltdown of 2007–08. As consumers began to default on their mortgages for various reasons, the flow of investment income to those who had purchased the pooled mortgages began to dry up. Since this investment income flow originated with consumers' mortgage payments, when those payments ceased, the resulting investment income also ceased. Mortgage-backed securities became known as "toxic assets," jeopardizing those who had invested in them, as well as the financial institutions and agencies that had bundled them.

BOND RATINGS AND INFORMATION

With all the choices in the bond market, judging risk can be pretty overwhelming. However, investors do not have to pick bonds at random and hope for the best. There are rating services (most notably, Moody's Investors Services, Fitch IBCA, and Standard & Poor's) that rate bonds on the assessment of the ability of the issuing entity to repay the bond. Each of the services uses a different rating scheme that is similar to the one below:

MOODY'S INVESTORS SERVICES BOND RATING CODES

Aaa	Highest quality; least amount of risk
Aa	High quality; considered safe. Aaa and Aa bonds are called high-grade bonds.
A	Upper-medium quality; have many attractive elements
Baa	Medium grade; bonds Baa and above are considered "investment grade."
Ba	Somewhat speculative (risky)
B	Low grade; speculative
Caa	Low grade; possibility of default
Ca	Low grade; might recovery some of investment
C	High probability of default; recovery of investment unlikely

Bonds that are rated Baa and above are called *investment grade bonds*. Bonds rated Ba and below are called *"junk"* or *"high yield"* bonds. As you have probably figured out, the coupon rates for these different levels of bonds varies, with the lowest coupon rate associated with Aaa bonds and the rate increasing as the bond rating falls.

Information about all types of bonds can be found in the financial section of newspapers or online. Bond tables will contain information like the following:

BOND	CUR YLD	VOL	CLOSE	% NET CHG
Pfizer, Inc. 4.65 18	4.096	32	103.723	+1.3
General Electric 5.0 13	2.359	180	107.301	—
Conoco Phillips 4.75 14	2.632	2	107.755	−2.25

The first column contains three pieces of information. The first is the bond name. Bonds are listed alphabetically by the entity's abbreviation. A corporation's abbreviation for its stock is not necessarily the same as for its bonds. The number immediately following the name is the coupon, or interest rate, on the bond. This rate is expressed as a percentage of the face value of the bond. Corporate bonds typically have a face value of $1,000, so a coupon rate of 4.65 percent means the annual interest payment on the bond will be $46.50. The coupon rate is followed by the year the bond will mature. By convention, only the last two digits of the year of maturity are shown. For example, the table above shows that bonds issued by Pfizer, Inc. have a coupon rate of 4.65 percent and will mature in 2018.

The second column contains information on the current yield. This is the return an investor would get if the bond was purchased at its current price, the close price listed in the next column. Notice that the coupon rate and the yield are not the same thing. Let us use the example of General Electric in the table above to reinforce this point. Remember that the coupon rate is the stated interest rate as a percentage of the face value. A bond's yield, however, is a very different thing. A bond's yield depends upon the price you pay for the bond. If you pay less than face value, then the yield on the bond will be higher than the coupon rate because at maturity you will receive the last interest payment plus the face value of the bond. If you paid less than par value, then the difference between par and what you paid is an additional return. On the other hand, if you must pay more than face value for a bond, (for example, you pay $1,073.01 as in the case of General Electric) you are paying $1,073 for a $1,000 bond. Why would you do that? To get the 5 percent interest ($50) payment that the bond carries. So, you receive 5 percent interest on the basis of the face value, but at maturity when you receive the face value of $1,000, that is $73 less than what you paid for it. So your total return, including the 5 percent interest payments and the fact that you will be paid less at maturity than what you paid for it, nets out to a total return of 2.359 percent.

Finally, the last column shows the net change in the bond price from the close of the previous trading day. These figures are expressed in either dollars and cents or a percentage change. In our example, Conoco Phillips' bond price fell by 2.25 percent from the previous day's trading.

The graph on page 59 shows the yield for different kinds of bonds over time.

The blue line is the yield on a 10-year Treasury bond. The red line is the yield on a corporate bond with a rating of Baa, while the purple line represents the "spread," or difference between the two. Bond prices peaked during

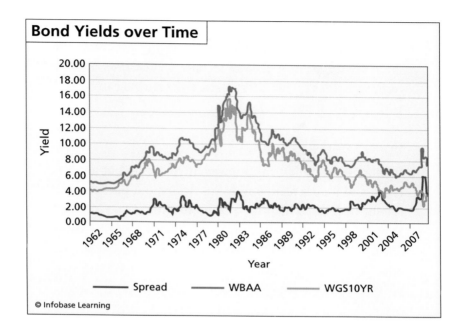

Bond Yields over Time

1980, during a recession that had extremely high inflation associated with it. In periods of high inflation, bond
yields are also high because interest rates not only reflect
the return of the investment, but inflation rates as well.

BONDS AND TIME HORIZON

Like certificates of deposit, time horizon has a lot to do
with a bond's interest rate. If you buy a bond that matures
in a short period of time (like a Treasury bill), you will
probably earn a lower rate of return than a bond that
matures in five years. Why? When you buy a longer-term
bond, you are locking yourself into an interest rate and
opening yourself up to interest rate risk—the risk that interest rates could increase during the time period that you
are locked into a lower rate. You are also exposed to inflation risk if your locked in rate does not keep pace with
inflation. So, longer term securities come with substantial

risk attached. Therefore, in order to persuade investors to purchase longer term bonds, the issuer must increase the interest rate as an incentive to take on the risk. Shorter term securities do not carry these risks and so can be sold with a lower interest rate.

Bond Laddering

If short term bonds pay a lower interest rate but are less risky, and longer term bonds are riskier, but pay a higher rate of interest, which type of bond should you choose? How do you balance the risk and the return? The good news is that you do not have to make a choice—you can have your low risk and your high return, too. You can do this by what is called *bond laddering*. Bond laddering means that you buy a series of bonds with different maturities that fit within your time frame. Let us do an example. Assume that you have a 10-year time frame; that is, you plan on a 10-year portfolio. To construct a laddered bond portfolio, you would buy bonds with maturity dates over that time span—maturing in one, two, three, up to 10 years. Therefore, when you construct your portfolio, you will have 10 different maturity dates for your bonds. At the end of one year, your one-year bonds have now matured, your two-year bonds will mature in one more year, your three-year bonds in another two, and so on. So, when your one-year bond matures and you are paid the final interest payment plus the par value, what do you do with the money? If you want to preserve the ladder, you take the money and buy bonds maturing in 10 years. Remember that you no longer have bonds that will mature in 10 years because your 10 year bonds now have *nine* more years until maturity, creating an opening at the 10 year rung on your ladder. So, as your bonds mature, you put the money back into the ladder by buy-ing bonds that mature in 10 years. This method provides you the benefits of both higher returns (you hold bonds up to 10 years in maturity) and lower risk (you also hold bonds that mature in the short term). Bond laddering is shown by the following graphic. Each color represents a bond of a specific maturity. After the end of the first year, each bond "moves" down the ladder, creating an opening at the top, the longest maturity, which is replaced by the maturity of the bottom-most bonds.

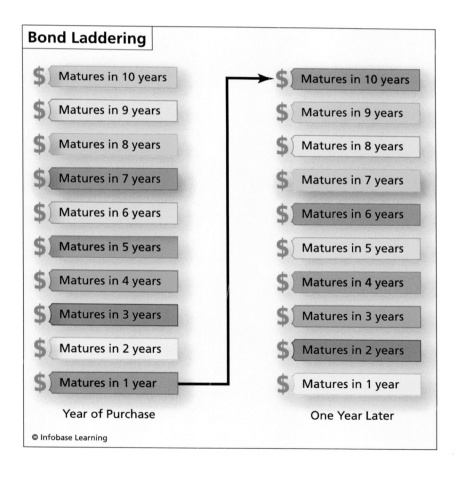

Bond Laddering

Year of Purchase	One Year Later
$ Matures in 10 years	$ Matures in 10 years
$ Matures in 9 years	$ Matures in 9 years
$ Matures in 8 years	$ Matures in 8 years
$ Matures in 7 years	$ Matures in 7 years
$ Matures in 6 years	$ Matures in 6 years
$ Matures in 5 years	$ Matures in 5 years
$ Matures in 4 years	$ Matures in 4 years
$ Matures in 3 years	$ Matures in 3 years
$ Matures in 2 years	$ Matures in 2 years
$ Matures in 1 year	$ Matures in 1 year

© Infobase Learning

Summary

When is a 5 percent return not necessarily a 5 percent return? In the world of bonds. Sorting through the ins and outs of the bond market can be challenging. Because bond prices are set by the market, a bond's yield to maturity might be different than the stated return as prices are bid up or down. While bonds typically have a reputation of being relatively safe, as we have seen, bonds are not without risk. Bond risk varies with the issuing entity and the time horizon. The risk/return trade-off can be somewhat ameliorated with the construction of a bond ladder, allowing the investor to benefit from both the returns on long-term bonds and the safety of short-term bonds.

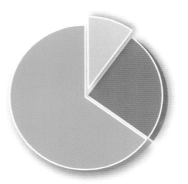

4

The Stock Market

Probably everyone has some notion of what the stock market is. We have all seen television and movie depictions of wild, seemingly insane people on the floor of the stock market, screaming incomprehensible words and clutching handfuls of their hair in despair. Well, that is about right. As we will see, the reality of the stock market is much more complex, but the popular representation of the stock market approximates how the whole thing works. So let us take a closer look at what stocks are, how the stock market works and what leads these people to behave so strangely.

WHAT IS A STOCK?

When you own *stock,* you own part of the company that issued it. For that reason, stocks are also called *equities* (meaning ownership). If you own a share of Walmart stock, you are an owner of Walmart. You are not a very large owner of Walmart, but an owner, nonetheless. Before we get too far ahead of ourselves, let us take a little time to talk about why a company would want to sell off parts of itself to total strangers.

What if you had a great idea for a new product and wanted to start your own company to produce it? How would you go about doing it? One of the first things you would need to consider is how you would get the money to get things rolling. There are a lot of expenses that would need to be paid before you even start producing. You need to find a production location, you need to buy or lease some equipment, buy some raw materials, hire some workers. Starting a business takes a lot of money. If you are not independently wealthy, you will need to find someone to give you the money. One option is to ask a bank for a loan. Taking out a loan to cover all your expenses can be expensive (banks charge interest, after all) and risky—what if business is slow in the beginning and you miss a few months' payments?

Another option is that you could approach some individuals and pitch your idea to them. If they are interested and think your idea is a good one, they can finance the start-up of your company. These are called *privately-held companies* because the ownership of the company consists of those who started the company, employees, or private investors. Privately-held companies do not trade stock on a stock exchange—the ownership is all internal to the firm.

A disadvantage of a privately-held company is that the access to funds is limited to those individuals who have bought in to your firm—a finite pool of resources. Therefore, you might want to consider a third way you could raise funds for your company—offer some ownership shares in your company to the public at large by selling stock in your company. When you first offer your stock for sale to the public, it is called an *initial public offering,* an IPO. An IPO is when a stock is first introduced on the public stage. IPOs occur when a company is just being started, as in our example, or more commonly, when a privately-held company decides to "go public" in an effort to raise more money than exists internally for expansion, investment, or some other reason.

You could also interest some *venture capitalists* in your idea. Venture capitalists are individuals who invest money in new companies to help them get started. They typically require a large ownership share in return. The difference between venture capitalists and private investors is that the goal for venture capitalists is to eventually take the company public. Finally, you could borrow money from the public by issuing bonds. This process was described in detail in the previous chapter.

A BRIEF HISTORY OF THE STOCK MARKET

The stock market in the United States began around the same time as the beginning of the country as the colonial government, trying to finance the war, sold government bonds and notes. At around the same time, private banks, also wanting to raise money, began to issue shares of stock in their banks to wealthy individuals. This new market prospered to the extent that in 1792, several merchants formalized the market, calling it the New York Stock Exchange. The merchants agreed to meet on a daily basis to trade stocks and bonds. They met under a large tree at the end of a street that followed the original path of a 17th-century wall that marked the northern boundary of the Dutch settlement on Manhattan Island—"Wall" Street. When the country experienced its tremendous expansion

The main building of the New York Stock Exchange, designed by George B. Post, opened on April 22, 1903. *(Shutterstock)*

a few years later in the mid-1800s, companies needed to raise funds to expand their output to meet the growing demand. They looked to selling stocks, and this new market was firmly established as a means for companies to raise funds and for investors to make significant profits.

HOW A STOCK IS BORN

Because IPOs are the foundation of the market, let us spend a little more time to understand how this process works. Traditionally, when a company decides to go public, they must go through a series of steps:

1. The company selects an *underwriter.* This is an investment bank that takes the lead on steering the company through the process.

2. The company develops a *prospectus.* A prospectus is like an informational brochure about the company—the financial details, the strategy for growth, debt obligations, etc. The prospectus must be filed with the *Securities and Exchange Commission* (SEC), the government agency that oversees securities markets (more about the SEC later in the chapter).

3. The underwriter assembles a *syndicate,* a group of other investment banks that will help sell the stock. Each member of the syndicate gets a proportion of the IPO to sell to its own clients. The syndicate members "test the waters," trying to determine what the demand will be for the company's stock.

4. The next step of the IPO process may seem a bit strange. The company's management team embarks on what is called "the road show." In the span of a week or two, the team travels to the major financial centers in the United States (other countries, too, if the stock will be an international offering) and meets with the major investors to sell their company's prospectus and drum up interest.

5. After the road show, the company and the underwriter decide on how many shares will be offered in the IPO and what the price will be. The price of the IPOs will be set lower than what the estimated price will be once

the stock starts trading publicly. After all, the big-money investors who buy the IPOs want to be able to turn around and sell the stocks to the public at a profit, so it is in their interests for the IPO price to be low. On the other hand, the company's only opportunity to make money selling stock is through the IPO. The proceeds of the IPO (minus the underwriter's fee) goes to the company issuing the stock. Once the IPO is concluded, however, the company does not make any additional money when the stock is sold by the big investors to other investors. The IPO is sold on what is called the primary market, and the issuing company gets the proceeds. Once the IPO is over, the stock is bought and sold on the secondary market, and the issuing company does not get any proceeds from all future sales of their stock.

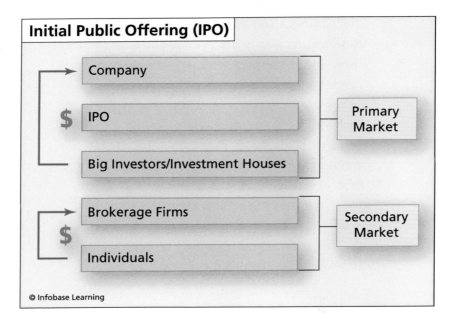

Initial Public Offering (IPO)

Company

$ IPO

Big Investors/Investment Houses

Primary Market

Brokerage Firms

$ Individuals

Secondary Market

© Infobase Learning

Dutch Auctions

The IPO process discussed above is the one that has been used for years. More recently, however, some companies (for example, Google) have changed the role of the underwriter and have relied more on the public to directly value their stock in what is known as a *Dutch auction*. To illustrate how a Dutch auction works, let us assume that a company, Giggle, wants to sell three million shares of its stock in an IPO. Investors who wish to purchase the stock must set up an account with Giggle's underwriter, an investment bank and get a bidder's identification number. The underwriter starts the auction by announcing a price (a very high one) for the stock (these auctions usually take place online), then waits to see if any bidder wants to buy shares at that price. If not, the underwriter lowers the price and waits for bidders to respond. The process is repeated until all the shares are sold. Here comes the interesting part: All the shares are then sold at the *lowest* price. Let us look at our company, Giggle.

DUTCH AUCTION TRANSACTIONS

Price	Number of Bidders	Total Shares Demanded	Cumulative Shares Sold
$100	0	0	0
$90	1	500,000	500,000
$80	3	1,500,000	2,000,000
$75	5	3,000,000	3,000,000
$70	8	4,000,000	4,000,000

The underwriter begins the bidding at $100. No registered bidders want the stock at that high price, so the underwriter lowers the price to $90. One investor is interested in buying 500,000 shares at $90 per share. Not all the stock is sold, however, so the underwriter lowers price again to $80, attracting three more buyers and selling a total of two million of the three million shares. This continues until the auction ends. The underwriter then looks at the auction results (this typically happens at the end of a period of time—results are not updated as the auction progresses). In our case, the stock is oversold—four million stocks are desired at the lowest price of $70, but only three million are available. So, the cutoff line is drawn at $75, where all the stocks are sold. The underwriter than notifies all the bidders of the selling price: $75. This lowest price is the price for all the bidders, even those who had been willing to pay $90 for a share of stock. The advantage of Dutch auctions is that IPOs are made more accessible to smaller investors than the traditional IPO offering process, which are reserved for big investors.

WHY OWN STOCKS?

Stocks are typically thought of as a long-term investment because of the volatility of the stock market. While it is true that the average return of the stock market over the long haul outperforms any other investment, in the short-term stocks can be very erratic:

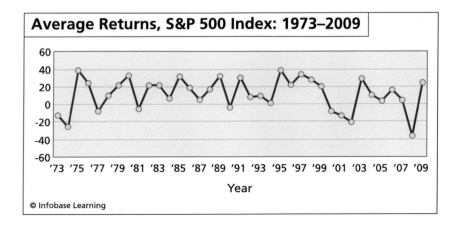

Average Returns, S&P 500 Index: 1973–2009

Year

© Infobase Learning

There are several things to note about this graph:

- On a year-to-year basis, returns vary quite a bit.
- When the market goes down, it is often only for one year.
- The market has many more positive-return years than otherwise—75 percent of the time the returns were positive.
- Of the years with positive returns, 78 percent are years with returns of 10 percent or higher.

As you can see, if your investing goals are fairly short-term, the stock market may not be the most appropriate place for your money—stock markets can fluctuated tremendously. When the stock market is experiencing rising prices (or the expectation of rising prices) we call it a *bull market.* Conversely, when stock prices are falling (or expected to fall), it is called a *bear market.* An easy way to remember the difference is to think of how bulls and bears attack their prey. Bulls thrust their horns upward when they attack; bears swipe their paws downward on their prey.

There are two possible returns on your investment when you own stock. The first possibility is a financial return called a *dividend.* If a company makes a profit, it has a couple of options of what to do with the money. It can keep the profit and invest it back into the company. This is called *retained earnings* and companies use retained earnings to expand, upgrade, etc. The second thing the profit-making company can do is to pay its stockholders all or a portion of the profits—this sharing of profits is called the dividend. The dividend does not have to be in the form of cash. A dividend can also be additional shares of stock in the company. Regardless of the form, it represents the company sharing its profits with the owners, the stockholders. Since companies do not always make a profit, or at least the same amount of profit, dividends often vary over time. The company's board of directors has the responsibility of deciding if a dividend is to be paid, and if so, how much and in what form. Dividends are usually paid quarterly. Not all companies pay dividends. For example, Microsoft did not pay a dividend to its stockholders until 2003, 28 years after its founding.

The second possible financial return on your stock investment occurs when you sell the stock. When you sell your shares of stock for more money than you paid for them, you have earned what is called a capital gain. A capital gain on any investment is simply the profit you earn: its current price minus what you paid to acquire it. Of course, you may also experience a *capital loss* if you cannot sell your stock for as much as you paid for it.

TYPES OF STOCKS

As discussed above, stocks are introduced in the primary market (when the issuing company gets the money from their sale), and then traded on the secondary market (when the profits from trading go to the people trading, not the issuing company). In addition, stocks usually (but not always) pay dividends to their shareholders. But all stocks are not the same. There are two major types of stock: *common* and *preferred.* The holders of common stock receive dividends (when the company issues them) that rise and fall with the profitability of the company. Common stockholders vote on the company's leadership (the board of directors) and company issues. Usually one share of common stock equates to one vote.

Preferred stock holders are guaranteed a dividend that is not directly linked to the company's profitability, but is either pegged to interest rates or is a specified dollar amount. Therefore, preferred stock represents a more stable investment than common stock. But, since these dividends are constrained, common stock may actually pay higher dividends in a good year. Preferred stockholders are paid dividends before dividends are paid to common stockholders. However, preferred stockholders do not get to vote on company issues or leadership. Some preferred stock can be converted to common stock at a price that is established at its issuance: *convertible preferred stock*. Therefore, preferred stock is still risky in that the principal is at risk if the company ceases to exist, but it is a more stable investment than common stock. For this reason, preferred stock is considered a cross between common stock and bonds.

STOCK MARKETS

Markets can take on many forms—the only requirement is that it provides a way for buyers and sellers to communicate and carry out their desire to exchange. The stock market is simply a way for those who want to sell shares of stock and those who want to purchase shares to find each other and conduct the exchange. Remember that when stocks are bought and sold on the stock market, that this is the secondary market—the company that issued the stock in the first place is not a participant in the stock market and does not gain from these transactions. They already received their gain from issuing the stock on the primary market. The other thing to know about the stock market is that it is not really "the" stock market—there are several markets.

New York Stock Exchange

The NYSE is probably the most widely known and is the oldest, having its origins back in the 1792 meeting of merchants that was discussed above. In addition, the NYSE is not for small companies. The exchange requires that its trading corporations have an outstanding share value of at least $100 million. This means that the value of the stock of the company that is held by the public (not the company itself), must be at least $100 million— called *capitalization*. These companies are called *large-cap companies* (large capitalization). In addition, in order to be a part of the NYSE, corporations must trade at least 100,000 shares per day. The NYSE is the largest stock exchange in the world in terms of dollar value of stocks traded.

Members of the NYSE are not the corporations themselves. Members (there are 1,366 of them) are stockbrokers, each member paying around $1.6 million (in 2010) for their "seat." Like the stocks that are traded, the price of seats on the Exchange has varied over the years, reflecting the attractiveness of the occupation of stockbroker. When the market is experiencing a decline (a bear market), being a stockbroker is not as desirable an occupation as it is when there is a bull market, so the price of a seat falls. When the market is bullish, being a stockbroker can be a very lucrative occupation, more people want to buy a seat, so the price of membership is bid up. The members of the Exchange carry out all the stock trades on the floor in New York City. This trading is what most people think of when they think of the stock market.

Arturo Di Modica designed the Charging Bull, a bronze sculpture installed near Wall Street. The bull represents financial aggressiveness, energy, and prosperity. When the stock market experiences rising prices, it is characterised as a bull market. *(Shutterstock)*

The NYSE contains several important indices that are used as general barometers of how the stock market is doing. A *stock index* is a way of measuring the value of many stocks that are similar in some way. The purpose of an index is to provide a way to track the ups and downs of the market with stocks that are similarly situated. For example, one of the most popular indices is the *Dow Jones Industrial Average* (DJIA), or the Dow, for short. The Dow tracks the performance of the 30 largest companies on the NYSE and is the most widely known index. Another index that is widely known is the *Standard and Poor's (S&P) 500*. This index is made up of the value of stocks of 500 companies on the NYSE.

Other Exchanges

While the NYSE is the oldest stock exchange and handles the largest companies, it is not the largest exchange, at least in terms of the number of shares traded. The National Association of Securities Dealers Automated Quotations *(NASDAQ)* trades the largest volume of stocks. Begun in 1971, the NASDAQ is home to a wide variety of technology stocks such as computer and software companies. In fact, not only does the NASDAQ specialize in the trading of technology stocks, but it is not a physical market—trading on the NASDAQ occurs electronically. The "virtual" nature of the exchange itself, combined with the fact that seats on the NASDAQ are not limited, means that the NASDAQ trades more stocks than the NYSE.

There are many stocks that do not meet the requirements to be traded on the NYSE. As a result, another stock exchange emerged long ago (during the Civil War) to provide a market for the stocks of smaller companies *(small-cap)*. The *American Stock Exchange (AMEX)* was a competitor of the NYSE for many years until it was acquired by the NYSE and renamed NYSE Amex Equities. The focus remains on small-cap stocks.

International Markets

Stock markets exist in many countries of the world, all with the same basic function. For example, the London Stock Exchange was founded to finance England's explorations, such as the East India Tea Company. Because the company could not finance its explorations itself, it sold shares of stock in the company, promising shares of profits when the ships returned. The Tokyo Stock Exchange is the second largest in the world in terms of market value (behind the NYSE), and houses the *Nikkei Index,* a stock market index similar to the Dow in the United States.

STOCK PRICES: WHY ARE THOSE PEOPLE SCREAMING AT EACH OTHER?

In order to understand how stocks are bought and sold in the stock market, you need to understand that, in one important respect, buying and selling stock is different from buying and selling about anything else. When you go to the store to buy something, the price is listed on the shelf, you go to the register, pay that price, and you own the good. You do not offer a lower price, nor does it ever occur to you to offer to pay a higher price for the right to buy the good. With stocks, the price that appears on the ticker (that continually flowing jumble of letters and numbers) does represent the price of the stock, but it is not the current price. It is the price that the stock sold for one second ago, or two seconds ago—sometime in the not-so-distant past. You may be able to get the stock for that price now, but then again, maybe not. Here is how it works.

The traders on the stock floor are holding *bid orders* and *ask orders*. Bid orders are instructions that have been phoned in from investors (operating through brokerage houses) to buy particular stocks at specified prices. Ask orders are similar instructions to sell stocks at specified prices. Let us go through a hypothetical example to see why the price of a stock is not necessarily the price you pay. At the opening bell on a particular trading day, the price of a single share of ABC stock is $100. This is the price that will appear on the ticker for ABC stock and that is the price now. Two seconds later, bid and ask orders for ABC stock start coming in to the floor traders. The difference between the ask price and the bid price is called the *spread*. If a bid order is $103 and an ask order is $105 (a spread of $2), the price of ABC stock will not change and will remain at $100 per share. Why? Because a bid order of $103 means that someone is willing to pay $103 per share, right now. But the ask order means that someone else is willing to sell ABC for $105 per share. They cannot agree on a price, so no transaction occurs, and the price stays at the opening price of $100. Another three seconds goes buy and a market order comes in. A *market order* is an instruction to the floor trader to exchange at whatever price is necessary to complete the deal. In our example, if the market order is a bid, the price of ABC stock will go to $105 per share—the sellers' price. If the market order is an ask, the price of ABC stock will go to $103 per share— the buyers' price. In either case, the price is different than the price that was displayed on the ticker just seconds ago ($100). In reality, these changes in price can occur many, many times in a single second, which explains all the yelling and seemingly insane behavior on the stock floor—the traders are executing hundreds of bid, ask, and market orders on hundreds of different stocks. Further,

View of the trading floor from the Member's Gallery of the New York Stock Exchange. *(Wikipedia)*

things do not stop once this one trade is made. The new price of ABC stock is higher than it was at opening, so this new, higher price may change future bids and asks throughout the day. No wonder things look crazy!

So now we know *how* stock prices get bounced around on the floor of the exchange, but *why* do they change? What determines the bids and asks? Stock prices are set in the same way that the price of anything is set: as a result of demand and supply. In the case of stocks, over the course of a day the supply of stock will not change.

There are X number of shares of stock out there for a company, and that number will stay the same in a day's time, probably longer. A company can issue more stock, or buy back some of its stock, thus increasing or decreasing the number of shares on the market, but for all practical purposes, we can think of the supply of stock as being fairly constant. That means that the fluctuation in stock prices is overwhelmingly due to changes in the demand for the stock. Remember that a company's stock price is an attempt by the market to determine a company's worth. Estimates of that worth can change depending on factors that are unique to the company, or because of external factors that the company cannot control. These are all things that will change the demand of a particular company's stock, thereby changing its stock price. If something about the company or external forces makes more people want to buy the stock, the price will be bid up. If the reverse is true and more people want to sell the stock, the price will fall.

Stock Price

The most important determinant of a company's stock price is the company's earnings. Companies issue earnings reports on a quarterly basis. However, the stock price of a company does not always change when a good (or bad) earnings report comes out. If earnings is the most important determinant of the price, why would price not change when earnings do? The reason has to do with expectations. Most people do not understand how important the role of expectations—people's beliefs—is in powering the stock market. Let us say you believe that 3-D television is the wave of the future, so you think investing in companies that make plastic 3-D glasses is a sure-fire winner. You are probably not the only one thinking along these lines. When you and everyone else who believes the same thing you do starts buying the stock of 3-D glasses producing firms, their stock prices will be pushed up— demand for the stock has increased. Remember, there has not been any increase in demand for 3-D *glasses* for home use, just an increase in demand for the stock of these companies. You and other like-minded investors just *think* there will be a big market for the product sometime in the future. But because you have acted on your beliefs, or expectations, the result is that the stock price of these companies has been pushed higher—just as if their earnings from selling 3-D glasses have gone up. Except they have not. Also remember that the company does not get the proceeds from the buying and selling of stock in the secondary market. So if you are correct and eventually these companies do start experiencing an increase in earnings because the sale of glasses has gone up, their earnings will just be catching up to their stock price. In other words, their increased earnings will have already shown up in the form of higher stock prices when they were bid up as a result of your expectations. The bottom line is this: Good (and bad) earnings reports only affect stock prices when the news is unexpected. If earnings reports are *expected* to be good (or bad), that expectation is already reflected in the stock price before the report comes out as investors act on their beliefs. If a report contains *unexpected* news (again, either good or bad), the stock price will change. For example, if a company reports better-than-expected earnings, its stock price will increase.

A related factor affecting stock prices is analysts' reports. Analysts from major investment banks and brokerage houses track stocks and issue regular reports on the market and individual stocks. When analysts give high recommendations to particular stocks, the demand for those stocks is likely to increase. Of course, these recommendations are based, in large part, on the company's earnings.

When a company announces a management team change, it will often change its stock price. If the changes are viewed to be good ones, the stock price will usually rise with these sorts of announcements. If there has been a technological advance in an industry, the companies within that industry will often see an increase in their stock prices as investors are predicting strong growth. This is true for drug companies as well—any company who relies on research and development.

If a large institution (investment or brokerage house) submits a bid or ask concerning a particular stock, the size of the order alone can change the stock price, but it can also be seen as a signal to others in the market. For example, if a large investment house submits an ask on a stock, others in the market might interpret this action to mean that the investment house thinks that earnings (and therefore, stock prices) of the company have peaked, so they are trying to get rid of their stocks at the high price before the prices start down again.

There are other factors that influence stock prices that are not specific to one company—economic-wide factors. For example, interest rates in the economy can affect stock prices in several ways. First, if interest rates are high, companies may find borrowing an expensive undertaking. When borrowing becomes more expensive, the increased interest payments can reduce profits, thus reducing the stock price. Interest rates can also affect stock prices indirectly. High interest rates are often associated with reduced consumer spending, and reduced consumer spending can result in lower company profits—leading to lower stock prices. Finally, when interest rates are high, investors may be tempted to shift their investment dollars away from lower-performing stocks to higher-return investments paying higher interest rates, like bonds.

In our global economy, the activities in other countries can affect stock prices in the United States. If the Nikkei Index falls dramatically, for example, it may cause a sharp drop in stock prices here and in other countries. Part of this is due to expectations, again. If investors see the fall in stock prices in Japan, they may expect prices to follow suit here, and react by selling off a lot of their shares (reducing demand). We see again the power of expectations. By anticipating a reduction in stock prices and then acting on that information, investors bring about the very reduction they feared. The other reason a drop in the Nikkei could affect our stock market depends upon how reliant we are on exports to Japan. If another country is experiencing a recession, their stock market is slumping, and their unemployment is high, their citizens will be buying less of all goods and services, including those that they import. The American companies providing those imported goods and services will experience a drop in profits, reducing their stock prices.

Now it is time to buy a stock. How do you choose which one to buy? To a large extent, it depends on what kind of investor you are, what you want your investment to do for you. Many stocks' prices reflect what investors think about the companies' potential for growth. Investors put their money in these stocks because they expect the stocks to become more valuable over time as the companies become more profitable. These stocks are called, not surprisingly, *growth stocks,* with the companies expected to grow at the rate of 15 percent or more per year.

Investors choosing growth stocks are most interested in the appreciation of the stocks' value over the years—the capital gain they can realize when they sell the stock. Therefore, growth stocks are most attractive to investors with long time horizons.

Value investors look for the bargains in the stock market, stocks whose prices have fallen because of a temporary (correctable) problem. Therefore, the price of *value stocks* is lower than what it will be after the problem is fixed. For example, if a company's management team has been replaced because the old team made a series of poor business decisions, the stock in that company is probably

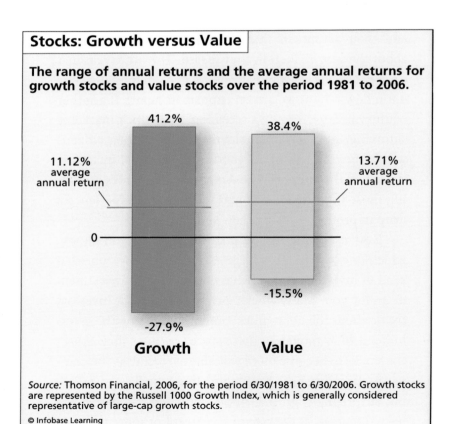

Stocks: Growth versus Value

The range of annual returns and the average annual returns for growth stocks and value stocks over the period 1981 to 2006.

41.2%

38.4%

11.12%
average
annual return

13.71%
average
annual return

0

-15.5%

-27.9%

Growth

Value

Source: Thomson Financial, 2006, for the period 6/30/1981 to 6/30/2006. Growth stocks are represented by the Russell 1000 Growth Index, which is generally considered representative of large-cap growth stocks.

© Infobase Learning

priced fairly low because of the mistakes of the previous team, but the price is poised to increase.

Still other investors are not as interested in the appreciation of the value of their stocks as they are in the dividends that a stock pays out. These investors are looking for steady, consistent dividend payouts for as long as they own the stock, not a gain when they sell the stock. These investors are interested in larger companies with a strong history of being able to continue to pay dividends through all kinds of market swings.

MEASURES OF STOCK PERFORMANCE

Regardless of the kind of investor you are and what kind of stock you are looking for, how do you know if the stock is overpriced, underpriced, or about right? There are several measures of stock performance that investors look at in determining whether to buy a stock.

> *Price-to-earnings ratio* (P/E): This ratio is computed by dividing a company's stock price by its earnings per share. The earnings figure is usually based on the company's previous 12-month earnings report. For example, if the stock price is $50 and the earnings per share is $5, the P/E ratio is 10 ($50/$5). This ratio means that investors are willing to pay $10 (in stock price) for every $1 the company earns. For this reason, the P/E ratio is also called the "multiple." In other words, the higher the P/E ratio, the more investors are willing to pay for each $1 of company earnings—the expectations for company earnings are high. Sometimes these expectations pay off; sometimes they do not. Very high

P/E ratios indicate stocks that are considered fairly risky. However, P/E ratios differ across industries. For example, P/E ratios of technology companies are usually higher than those in an industry like utilities because technology companies are more likely to be growth industries. Therefore, comparisons of P/E ratios across industries is not useful.

Price-to-sales (P/S): This ratio is formed by dividing a company's stock price by the sales per share figure. Sales usually do not change as much over time as earnings do, so some investors think the P/S ratio is a better indicator of the health of the company than the P/E ratio. In addition, if a company loses money, there is no earnings figure to use to compute the P/E ratio, so the P/S ratio can be used whether the company earns a profit or not.

Price-to-book (P/B): A company's *book value* is the company's assets minus their liabilities. The P/B ratio is formed by dividing the stock price by the book value per share.

BUYING AND SELLING STOCK

You understand how the market works, you have researched your stock, and now you are ready to actually jump into the market. How do you do that? The first step is to set up an account with an online broker (some well-known ones include Charles Schwab, ETrade, T.D. Ameritrade) Once your account is set up, you can buy, sell and engage in short sales.

When you want to buy stock, you specify how many shares you want to buy. You can either instruct the broker to buy at the best price in effect when you place the order (this is the market order we talked about earlier), or you can set a maximum price that you are willing to pay for the stock. This is called a *limit order.* Limit orders are helpful when stock prices are moving very quickly. Because the price of a stock can change many times in matter of just a few seconds, you may think the stock is trading for $50 a share, but within just a few seconds the price may be pushed to $75 a share by the time your order is received. If you have only placed a market order, you will be paying $75 a share when you thought you were only paying $50. If you had placed a limit order of $50, you would not buy any shares at $75, but your limit order would remain open (for some period of time) until the price falls back down to $50. If it does not fall back down to $50 within the period of time, you have not purchased any stock.

When you buy stock it is not always necessary for you to have all the money on hand in order to complete the purchase. You can sometimes buy a stock on *margin,* meaning you can pay part of the purchase price and borrow the rest from your broker, using your investment as collateral. Here is how buying on margin can work in your favor. Let us say you would like to buy some stock whose price is $100 per share. You have $500 to invest, so if you pay in cash you can buy five shares. If the stock rises in value in the next year to $150, your stock is now worth $750, so you made $250, or a 50 percent return. If instead of buying the stock with cash, you had bought it on margin, you could have purchased 10 shares (you put up half of the money and you borrow the other half from your broker). The increase in value of the stock over the next year means that your stock is worth $1,500. You pay back your broker the $500 (plus interest) you borrowed (the margin), leaving you with $1,000. Since you started with $500 of your own money, so you have made $500, or a 100 percent return, twice as much as you did when you paid cash. Using margin increases your purchasing power, allowing you to buy more stock than you otherwise could. This is referred to as using *leverage*.

The problem with buying on margin comes when the price of your stock goes down. In our example above, if the price of the stock falls from its original price of $100 to $70, the stock you bought for $500 will now be worth only $350, and you will lose $150 if you paid cash—a 30 percent loss. If you bought the stock on margin, your stock would be worth $700, down from $1,000. You still owe your broker $500 (plus interest), leaving you with $200. You put $500 of your own money into the purchase, so your net loss is $300, a 60 percent loss. Leverage magnifies both gains and losses. In addition to the risk associated with borrowing the money from your broker, your broker can sell the stock you bought on margin ("your" stock) at any time and without any notice.

When you want to sell some stock, a similar process occurs. You enter either a market order (sell at whatever the current price is at the time the order is received), or a limit order (a minimum price at which you are willing to sell the stock). As with buy limit orders, this option is helpful when the stock price is moving quickly to prevent you from selling at a price that is lower than what you thought.

If you want to sell stock, one approach can be to say that you do not want to sell the stock if it falls below a minimum price, say $40 a share. This is the sell limit order discussed above. On the other hand, sometimes investors place sell stops. A *sell stop* is an order to sell the stock if it falls below a certain level. Sells stops are attempts at minimizing the loss if you have made a poor choice in stock selection. For example, if you bought the stock at $50 a share, you could set a sell stop at $35 a share. If the price of the stock starts falling, your order is to sell your shares when the price hits $35 a share. You want to cut your losses rather than risk the stock going down even further. But as with many things, timing is everything. Let us say your stock is heading downhill. You have a sell stop in place for $35, but the stock price has not fallen that far yet. At the closing bell, the stock price is $37. Since this price is above your sell stop, your stock has not been sold. Overnight, news hits that the issuing company is being investigated for accounting irregularities. When the stock market opens the next day, your stock is now selling for $20 a share. Unfortunately, the price of $20 is all you are going to get for your stock. In other words, a sell stop does not guarantee that you will be able to sell your stock for the price you have set.

Now you know how to buy stock and then sell the stock that you own. But did you know that you can also sell stock that you do *not* own? That's right—you can sell stock that belongs to someone else, specifically, your broker. Here is how it works. You borrow some shares of stock from your broker and then sell them. Let us say you borrow 100 shares and sell them for $50 per share. You now have $5,000, but you still owe your broker 100 shares of stock. You are hoping that the price of the stock will go down. Why? Because if the price goes down, to say $40 a share, you can buy 100 shares for $4,000, give the shares back to your broker, and you have just made $1,000. This is called *selling short,* or having a *short position.* Investors who sell short are counting on the market being bearish—

Warren Buffet

Warren Buffet is one of the most successful investors in the world, beginning his career at age six when he brought a six-pack of sodas for a quarter and resold them for a nickel each. He graduated from the University of Nebraska-Lincoln in three years, applied to Harvard Business School and was rejected because he was too young. He was admitted to Columbia and became a student of a pioneering investor, Ben Graham. Buffet discovered that Graham was the chairman of a small, unknown insurance company called Geico. He visited the company and spent four hours talking to the vice-president for finance. Buffet would eventually acquire Geico.

Buffet started developing his approach to investing by looking at how companies were managed, rather than the numbers the companies generated. He began is own investing company in 1956, and began accumulating a return of 251 percent at a time when the Dow was up only 74.3 percent. His company continued to grow, and he eventually took control of a company called Berkshire Hathaway. Berkshire Hathaway acquired many firms, and Warren Buffet began buying stock for his own personal portfolio. He concentrated on buying stock in companies that had undervalued stock, ignoring bubbles like the dot.com decline in the late 1990s. His investment strategy has endured, making his opinion so well-respected that just a rumor that Warren Buffet is buying a stock can send the stock's price skyrocketing.

Warren Buffet and President Barack Obama in the Oval Office on July 14, 2010 (Wikipedia)

stock prices going down. This is the opposite of being long in the market. If you have a *long position,* you buy stock with the expectation that the stock price will increase (being bullish). Buying long is the usual position for most investors.

With all this information, it might seem like the stock market is hopelessly complicated—a labyrinth that no one can penetrate. There are individuals, however, who have done very well navigating all the ins and outs of the stock market. Perhaps the most notable among these is Warren Buffet.

READING THE STOCK PAGE

Whether you are reading stock information in the newspaper or online, information will be presented similar to the following:

EXAMPLE OF STOCK INFORMATION

STOCK/SYMBOL	52-WEEK HI	LO	DIV	YLD %	P/E	VOL	CLOSE	NET CHG
Disney DIS	33.85	17.08	0.35	1.04%	19.22	16.72 M	33.64	−0.14

The first column shows the company name, along with the stock market symbol. The second column shows the stock's high and low price from the previous 52-week period. The next column shows the amount of the last dividend payout (per share), while the fourth column presents the dividend as a percentage of the closing price (0.35/33.64). The price/earnings ratio is presented next, indicating that investors pay $19.22 for every $1 in company earnings. On the day of reporting 16 million shares of Disney stock traded. The closing price of the previous trading day was $33.64, representing a decrease in price of $0.14 from the prior day's close.

REGULATION OF THE STOCK MARKET

In the aftermath of the stock market crash of 1929, it became apparent that greater governmental oversight was needed in the securities market. In an effort to address these laxities, the U.S. Securities and Exchange Commission was established. The primary purpose of the SEC is to ensure that all investors have access to full and truthful information about companies before they invest in them. To that end, the SEC requires that public companies disclose their annual reports to the public. The SEC also regulates the behavior of stock brokers and others who advise investors. If it finds violations, the SEC can impose fines, order companies to cease certain behaviors, or even initiate criminal proceedings. There are four violations that are most commonly found by the SEC:

- Insider trading. Information about a company is supposed to be available to everyone. When an individual knows more about a company's operations, knows that this information will change the value of the company's stock, and acts on this information for financial gain, they have committed *insider trading*. For the most part, the people who would know the most about the company are those in the company's management and on the board of directors—those "inside" the company.

- Inaccurate information. If a company omits or misrepresents important information in their publicly released documents, they may have violated SEC regulations.

- Price fixing. *Price fixing* occurs when an attempt is made to interfere with the market-determined price of a stock. For example, if an individual uses his/her influence to persuade others that the price of a stock will fall (saying that the company will be investigated, for instance), in order to be able to buy shares of the stock at artificially low prices, this violates SEC rules.

- Theft of clients' funds.

AND FINALLY, A BIT OF HISTORY

You have heard of the Great Depression and the stock market crash that accompanied it. With the recent financial collapse of 2008–09, many wonder if the same forces were at work and if a stock market crash like that of 1929 could happen again. We cannot make an informed judgment about the likelihood of a repetition if we do not know exactly what happened in '29.

The era of the 1920s was a period of tremendous expansion. Incomes were rising, more and more Americans were purchasing houses and cars on credit—life was good. The Federal Reserve Bank had been created (in 1913), but was not a major player in the economy. The stock market was booming, with participation largely restricted to the very rich. These investors found that the stock market was a good way to make even more money. They were particularly fond of buying stock on margin. As discussed above, buying on margin simply means borrowing money from your broker to purchase stock. Back in 1929, the Securities and Exchange Commission did not yet exist, so there were no regulations about margin buys. Investors could buy stock on a 90 percent margin. This means that an investor could buy $1 million of stock by only putting up $10,000 of his/her own money and borrowing the other $990,000 from the broker. This arrangement is all well and good as long as everything is running smoothly and the economy is growing.

Toward the end of the 1920s, the country entered a recession. There was nothing special about this recession; it seemed a recession like many others that had come before. As with any recession, consumer incomes started to fall, causing consumer spending and company profits to fall. So what caused this run-of-the-mill recession to become the Great Depression? There are many answers, but an important one resides in the stock market. The stock market had been booming, but much of the increase in stock prices was a result of a speculative bubble. A *bubble* results when the price of an asset (in this case, stocks) increases rapidly for reasons other than an actual increase in value. In other words, stock prices were rising because groups of investors were buying and selling each other's stock. Stock prices are supposed to rise when the underlying value of the company has increased. In this case, the companies were not improving their products, their management teams were not becoming more efficient; they were not doing anything that would increase the actual value of the company. Their stock prices, however, were rising quickly only because investors were buying up the stocks, hoping to make a very large return (speculating). Because the run-up in prices was not based on anything substantive (making it a bubble), when the economy entered into a recession and company earnings started to fall, brokers started to call in all of those margin orders. Suddenly, large investors were facing margin calls from their brokers of 90 percent of the stock prices. Where could they get this money? To the extent they had the money at all, they got it from their banks. Soon, banks ran out of money. There was no deposit insurance then, so when large amounts of money was withdrawn from banks it caused a run on the banks.

Stock margins are now regulated and can go no lower than 50 percent (the amount of a stock's price that the investor has to pay cannot fall below 50 percent). Companies are required to divulge their financial situation when there were no such requirements in 1929. Insider trading and other behaviors that helped to inflate the speculative bubble in 1929 are prohibited today. That being said, speculative bubbles in other financial markets are not only possible, but do exist, as recently seen by the real estate bubble that preceded the financial meltdown of 2007–08.

SUMMARY

From a distance, the stock market looks like a wild ride. But there is a method to the madness. The chaos on the floor of the stock exchange is simply traders acting on orders, reflecting shifting demand for various stocks. It is much livelier than your grocery store, perhaps, but the basic market mechanics are the same. In spite of the chaos, investments in stocks continue to outperform other forms of investments over the long haul.

5

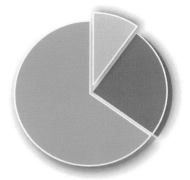

Other Investment Options

The previous chapters have covered some common saving and investment instruments: bank accounts, bonds, and stocks. These instruments are not the only options, however. This chapter covers some of those other choices, some of which are just combinations of the securities we have covered in the previous chapters.

MONEY MARKET FUNDS (MMFS)

The first thing you need to know about *money market funds* is that they are not the same as money market accounts. Money market accounts were covered in the first chapter as another savings instrument available at banks. Money market accounts are insured by the FDIC, just as savings and checking accounts are. Money market funds are not insured and often have minimum deposit requirements.

So what are money market funds? As discussed in the chapters on stocks and bonds, when corporations need to raise cash, they can issue stocks and/or bonds; when the government needs to raise funds (federal, state, or local), it can issue bonds. But issuing stocks and bonds is a long-run undertaking. When an entity issues a bond, for example, it is typically a long-term security. What does a corporation or a government do when it needs cash for just a short amount of time? It issues money market instruments. These instruments are like bonds in that they are IOUs, promising to pay the money back. Unlike bonds, money market instruments are of very short duration. Money market funds are typically issued by levels of government and very large corporations, those who can be relied upon (for the most part) to be able to pay back the debt.

When you buy a money market fund, you are actually buying shares of the fund. Usually the price of each share of a fund is priced at $1, so if you invest $100 in a money market fund, you have purchased 100 shares. Of course, you are not the only person investing in this particular money market fund—many others are investing in the same fund. The fund manager pools all of the money from you and other investors and gives it to governments and large corporations in the form of loans. Since these are loans, not only do governments and large corporations give you your money back (although it is not guaranteed), you also get the interest that they are paying to borrow the money from you. These interest payments are paid to you in the form of dividends. You can receive your dividends in the form of a check, or you can choose to have your dividends reinvested in the fund.

To decide which money market fund to invest in, you can compare the yield of various funds. The yield of a fund is the dividend per share divided by the share price. Since the price per share is usually $1, the yield is simply the dividend per share. Another factor in the decision of what money market fund to invest in is the tax status of the fund. There are two major types of funds: taxable and tax-exempt.

Taxable Money Market Funds

As you might expect, given the name, with taxable money market funds, you pay taxes on the dividends you receive from the fund. The most common types of taxable money market funds are the following.

- Corporate money funds are invested in securities (short-term debt) that are issued by large corporations. There is always a risk that the corporation will not be able to repay the loan (this happens very infrequently). In addition, dividends from corporate money funds are subject to state tax as well as federal tax. Because of the additional tax liability and the risk, the yield of these funds tends to be a bit higher than that of the next two funds.

- U.S. Treasury money funds are invested in Treasury bills and are risk-free (see chapter 3 for a description of these securities). The dividends are subject to federal tax. They may also be subject to state tax—rules vary by state.

- U.S. government money funds are invested in other kinds of government and government agency instruments. These securities are not guaranteed by the federal government (as

T-bills are) and are therefore slightly riskier than Treasury money funds. Again, whether the dividends are subject to state tax or not varies by state.

Tax-Exempt Money Market Funds

The dividends from tax-exempt funds are not subject to federal income tax, but may or may not be subject to other taxes. Because they are tax exempt, the dividends are typically lower than is the case with taxable funds.

- Federal tax-exempt money funds are invested in instruments issued by various levels of government (for example, states and cities). The dividends from these funds may be subject to state and local tax.
- Double tax-exempt money funds are invested in instruments issued by one state (or other government entity), making the dividends exempt from both federal and state taxes.
- Triple tax-exempt money funds are invested in instruments issued by a single city; the dividends are exempt from federal, state, and local taxes.

Therefore, the choice of money market fund depends not only the yield, but also on your tax bracket.

MUTUAL FUNDS

In chapter 1 we introduced the idea of diversification as a way to manage risk. Investing in a *mutual fund* is an easy way to diversify because a mutual fund pools the money from many, many investors. This pooled money is then used to purchase a variety of instruments: stocks, bonds, and money market funds. Whatever the type of mutual fund, there are fees involved with its management. These fees make up the expense ratio, which lowers your return. Mutual funds can have an additional expense, called a *load*. A load is a fee that is charged every time you buy or sell shares in the fund. If a fund is a *no-load fund,* no fees are charged for making these transactions.

One type of mutual fund is a stock mutual fund where your dollars are pooled with other investors' and a variety of stocks are purchased by the fund manager. While different mutual funds have different objectives (growth, for example), they all share the common characteristic of buying many stocks to populate the fund. If you buy just one company's stock, or even two or five, if these companies suffer losses and their stock prices fall, your investment also takes a hit. On the other hand, if your money is pooled with hundreds of other investors' money and then invested in a large number of stocks, if one or two of the companies' stock prices decrease, you still have money invested in other companies that have not suffered losses. Therefore, your investment does not fall as much as if all your money was tied up in one or two stocks.

The performance of the stock mutual fund is largely dependent upon the stock fund manager. With *actively managed funds,* the stock fund manager picks the stocks to include in the fund. With other types of funds, however, the stock fund manager does not play such an active role. With *index funds,* the job of the manager is not to pick the individual stocks from the entire population of stocks, but to simply include the stocks that are contained in a particular index, such as the S&P 500 (see chapter 2 for a description of stock indices). Since the manager's role in an index fund is more passive than that in an actively managed fund, the fees associated with an index fund are lower. As a general rule, however, index funds have performed as well or better than most actively managed funds that rely on the manager's expertise.

Mutual funds can also be made up of bonds, again representing the pooled investment money of many investors spread over many bonds. Bond funds vary by the entity that is issuing the bonds, following the same categories as those for money market funds above. The second difference among bond funds is in the length of time to bond maturity of the bonds in the fund. Bond funds that invest in bonds that mature in fewer than four years are called *short-term bond funds.* Bonds that mature in four to 10 years comprise *intermediate bond funds,* and *long-term bond funds* are made up of bonds that mature in more than 10 years.

RETIREMENT ACCOUNTS

One of the major things that people save for is retirement. You may think that a retirement account is something that people do not start worrying about until they are in the middle of their working lives. Sadly, this is true for a lot of people. What you need to know is that it is likely that these people will not have enough saved for their retirement and will be forced to work longer than they would like or live a dramatically different lifestyle than the one they had planned.

Retirement planning has changed over the years. It used to be that when someone went to work for a company, there was a pension plan that the company (and possibly, the employee) contributed to over the years. Upon retirement, the company would pay out a fixed amount every month. These pension plans are called *defined benefit plans* and made planning for retirement fairly easy since the monthly pension was guaranteed. Fewer and fewer companies are offering defined benefits plans, primarily because with these plans, the company has to absorb all the market risk. The company invests the funds that it will pay out to retirees, and when the market goes down, the company still has to pay out the same amount even though its returns have decreased. In an effort to relieve themselves of this downside risk, many corporations have changed to *defined contribution plans*. Defined contribution plans do not guarantee the monthly payments, they guarantee the monthly contributions. In other words, instead of an employee knowing that he/she will receive $700/month upon retirement under a defined benefits plan, he/she knows that the employer will contribute $50/month to a pension plan during years of employment. The amount that the retiree then gets upon retirement depends upon what the market has done in the interim. The employee, therefore, bears the market risk.

When planning for retirement, compound interest becomes particularly important (discussed in chapter 1) because of the long time horizon. Setting up and contributing to a retirement account should begin as soon as you are finished with your schooling and are receiving a steady income. You can do this in several ways.

401(k)s

Many employers offer opportunities for their employees to set up these tax-deferred accounts. When an employee makes contributions to a *401(k) plan*, these contributions are not treated as taxable income for federal tax purposes. For example, if you earn $50,000 a year and contribute $2,000 per year to a 401(k) plan, you are only taxed on $48,000 of income. The income you earn on the investment accumulates tax free. Upon retirement, however, the distributions from the plan are taxable. Some employers offer a "match," meaning that as long as the employee contributes some minimum amount, the company will match it (up to a limit). With *participant-directed plans,* the employee decides how these funds are to be invested, usually choosing among various mutual funds that focus on stock, bonds, or money market investments. Some 401(k) plans are *trustee-directed,* meaning that a trustee employed by the company makes the investment decisions. For employees of public schools and some other organizations, the retirement plans are called *403(b) plans.* They operate the same as 401(k)s.

If you need to make a withdrawal from your 401(k) before you reach the age of 59½, you must make a case for a hardship disbursement. Employers vary as to what the specific provisions are, but in general, when you withdraw funds early you must pay tax on the distribution, plus a 10 percent penalty on the withdrawn funds. If you need the money in your account, instead of withdrawing the money, you can borrow from your 401(k). You may be thinking, But it is my money! And you are right. You would essentially be borrowing from yourself, and the payments you make (both principal and interest) go back into your account. Again, the rules about borrowing vary among employers, but there are usually limits about how much you can borrow and the time period you have to pay the loan back.

Individual Retirement Accounts

If a company does not offer a 401(k) plan, employees can still save for retirement through privately held *individual retirement accounts,* or *IRAs.* (IRAs are also available to some employees who are covered separately by their employer's 401(k), but there are some restrictions). Contributions to deductible IRAs are treated the same as for 401(k) plans, reducing taxable income. There are income limits concerning whether the contributions are fully deductible, partially deductible, or not deductible at all (at higher income levels). There are also maximum annual amounts that can be contributed to an IRA ($5,000 in 2010). Like 401(k)s, the distributions of traditional IRAs are taxable as income at retirement. If you need to take your money out of a traditional IRA before you reach age 59½, you will have to pay the income tax on your balance, plus a 10 percent penalty on the money you withdraw early.

Another type of IRA is the newer, *Roth IRA*. With Roth IRAs, the contributions are not tax deductible. If you earn $50,000 per year and contribute $2,000 to a Roth IRA, you will still be taxed on the full $50,000. Once you make the contribution, however, the money in your Roth IRA will not be subjected to any other tax. Your investments grow tax-free, and your distributions at retirement are not taxed. You can also open a Roth IRA even if you have a retirement account through your employer. Like a traditional IRA, there are some restrictions about what your income can be to get the full tax benefits of contributions. This works on a sliding scale, so even if you earn too much to make a full contribution, you can still make a partial contribution as long as you earn less than maximum amounts that vary by single and married tax filers. With a Roth IRA, if you need to withdraw funds before you reach 59½, you can withdraw your *contributions* without any penalty whatsoever. If you withdraw the *interest* that you have earned, however, you must pay both the tax and the penalty.

Whether a particular investment is tax deferred or taxable can make a big difference in the accumulated amount. For example, let us assume that we invest $200 a month, or $2,400 a year, compounded monthly, for 20 years, earning 8 percent per year. The following graph shows the difference in accumulation for investments that are tax-deferred, tax-free, and taxable:

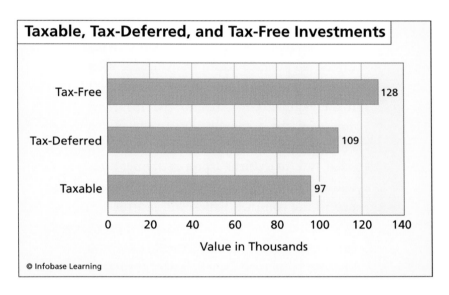

These data were generated assuming a 28 percent tax bracket—other tax brackets would change the results, but the main point remains: Choosing tax-exempt or tax-free investment can make a big difference in total investment value.

Annuities

Another vehicle that is available for retirement savings is an *annuity*. An annuity is an agreement between an individual and an insurance company. The individual pays the insurance company a lump sum or makes periodic payments to the insurance company over time. Upon retirement, the insurance company makes regular payments to the individual for the rest of his/her life. Interest earned on annuities are tax-deferred until payments are received. Unlike IRAs, annuities do not have caps on annual contributions, but there can be penalties for early withdrawals.

> *Fixed annuities:* The "fixed" portion of fixed annuities refers to the interest that is earned on the payments made to an insurance company. If you purchase a *fixed annuity,* you make regular payments to the insurance company, the company invests the money and guarantees that you will receive some fixed rate of return. Upon retirement you will receive a periodic payment that is specified in the contract, which will last the rest of your life. Some annuities also have provisions for extending the payments past your lifetime to named beneficiaries. Insurance companies are in business to make a profit, which they do when someone does not live as long as the insurance company expects. Conversely, if someone outlives the insurance company's expectations, forcing them to pay out for a longer period of time than expected, they suffer a loss. The insurance company expects that these opposite forces will balance out.
>
> *Variable annuities:* If you buy a *variable annuity,* you will be responsible for directing your money to various investment instruments. This is in contrast to fixed annuities, where

investment decisions are made by the insurance company. There is no guarantee of a payout with variable annuities—the amount you receive depends upon the rate of return on the investments you have chosen. Variable annuities also have high fees attached to them. Since you are directing your money to a mutual fund, you incur the fees associated with that fund(s). The money you are investing, however, is going through an insurance company first, so there are also fees associated with the insurance company's involvement.

Indexed Annuities: An *indexed annuity* is a hybrid of a fixed and variable annuity. With an indexed annuity, you can tie your return to the performance of a financial index, such as the S&P 500. Indexed annuity contracts typically specify a range within which returns can vary: a lower limit of zero (no negative returns), and an upper limit consistent with the average performance of the index. Therefore, an indexed annuity typically results in a higher rate of return than that of fixed annuities, while protecting (to a large extent) against the market risk inherent in variable annuities.

SAVING FOR COLLEGE

No, not your college—your future children's college. Like saving for retirement, time is on your side, so the earlier the start you get, the better off you will be. In fact, the time horizon for college savings is less than that for retirement—only 18 years for college, compared to your entire working life for retirement. Saving for college can be done with many of the saving and investment instruments already covered (savings bonds, mutual funds, etc.)

One of the newer instruments available specifically for savings for a college education is called a 529 plan. A *529 plan* is an educational saving plan offered by a state or an educational institution itself. Although many states offer these plans, your child does not have to be a resident of the state whose plan you enroll in, nor is your child required to attend college in that state.

There are two types of 529 plans. A *529 Savings Plan* works a lot like an IRA or 401(k), except that the contributions to the plan are not tax deductible. Once the contributions are made, however, the investments grow tax free, and when disbursements are made, they are also free of federal taxes. *Prepaid plans* allow you to prepay the tuition at a state's public institutions, allowing you to lock in tuition rates years before your child will be ready to enter college. Since tuition increases at an average rate of about 8 percent per year, this can represent a substantial savings. Prepaid plans have allowances that permit you to transfer the balance in the plan to another state or to a private institution if desired.

SUMMARY

Savings and investing decisions are puzzles with many pieces. Deciding on your savings goal is the easy part. To some extent, the type of investment vehicle you choose will be determined by your particular goal—529 plans are used for college savings, annuities are retirement instruments, etc. But you can save for college and retirement with other investments as well, and so you need to have a good understanding of what these choices are. You certainly do not need to be an expert in investments to manage your own savings effectively. However, you do need to understand the terminology, spend time investigating the instruments you are considering, and be consistent in carrying out your plan. After all, having all the knowledge in the world about investment options will not help you if you do not actually use it.

Test Your Knowledge

1. According to the Rule of 72, how long will it take a $7,200 deposit to double if the interest rate is 8?

    a. 100 months

    b. 9 years

    c. 9 months

    d. 90 months

2. Which of the following ranks savings instruments from lowest interest rate to highest (typically)?

    a. CD/money market account/savings account

    b. CD/savings account/money market account

    c. savings account/money market account/CD

    d. money market account/savings account/CD

3. The APR and APY on an investment

    a. are the same thing

    b. are different because they each use a different beginning balance in the computation

    c. are different because of the effects of compounding

    d. are the same thing only if the investment is for more than one year

4. If you keep your money in an FDIC-insured savings account, which type of risk are you exposed to?

 a. market risk
 b. interest rate risk
 c. inflation risk
 d. none—since the account is insured, you are protected from all risk

5. With a zero coupon bond

 a. you earn a 0 percent interest rate
 b. you do not receive interest payments over the life of the bond
 c. you do not make any money
 d. you receive interest payments over the life of the bond, but the bond has no value at maturity

6. A bond's yield to maturity

 a. is greater than its current yield when its price increases
 b. is less than its current yield when its price decreases
 c. is always the same as its current yield
 d. is the same as its current yield only when the bond's price is face value

7. Corporate bonds

 a. receive favorable tax treatment

   b. are issued when corporations need to raise money

   c. are about the same risk as government bonds

   d. usually pay a lower yield than government bonds

8. The returns an investor gets in the stock market

   a. are always larger than any other investment

   b. do not vary very much from year to year

   c. tend to stay negative for long periods of time

   d. are, on average, larger than other investments

9. The New York Stock Exchange

   a. only trades the stocks of large-cap companies

   b. trades more stocks than any other stock exchange in the world

   c. has unrestricted membership

   d. is not a physical location—all exchanges are conducted virtually

10. When you place a limit order

   a. you are limiting how many stocks you want to buy

   b. you are limiting the minimum price at which you are willing to sell your stock

   c. you are limiting the maximum price at which you are willing to buy stock

   d. you are limiting the number of times you buy stock during a single trading day

11. If you think that the price of a particular stock will go down

   a. you can still make money on that stock if you sell short
   b. you can still make money on that stock if you sell long
   c. you cannot make money—the only way to make money in the stock market is when stock prices increase
   d. you should buy now and sell at the lower price later

12. If you want to save for a child's college education, the best instrument for doing that is

   a. a Roth IRA
   b. a fixed annuity
   c. a 529 plan
   d. a taxable money market fund

Compare your work with the answer key found at the end of the Glossary section.

 Glossary

401(k) plan   A tax-deferred retirement plan offered by employers.

403(b) plan   A tax deferred retirement plan available to public employees.

529 plan   An educational savings plan offered by a state or educational institution.

529 prepaid plan   An educational savings plan whereby tuition is prepaid, locking in current tuition rate.

529 savings plan   An educational savings plan where the contributions are made with after-tax dollars, but the disbursements (and increase in value) are tax free.

actively managed fund   A stock mutual fund where the manager picks the stocks that are included in the fund.

American Stock Exchange (AMEX)   A stock exchange that trades small cap companies, it was acquired by the New York Stock Exchange.

annual percentage yield   The return on a savings instrument or investment that takes into account the cumulative effects of compounding.

annuity   A contractual agreement between an individual and an insurance company where the individual makes a lump sum or periodic payments. At retirement, the company makes regular payments to the individual.

ask order   An instruction from an investor to a broker to sell a stock at a particular price.

automatic teller machine (ATM)   A machine owned by financial institutions that provides banking services, such as cash withdrawals and deposits, to customers.

bear market   A term that is used to describe the stock market when stock values are declining.

beta   A measure of the variability of an investment's return; used as a relative measure of risk.

bid order   An instruction from an investor to a broker to buy a stock at a particular price.

board of governors   The decision-making body of the Federal Reserve, it is composed of the presidents of seven of the 12 regional Federal Reserve Banks.

bond   An IOU that is issued by a government or corporation to fund its operation.

bond laddering   The practice of owning bonds with maturity dates of varying length and replacing those that come due with others of the same maturity.

bond yield   Also called yield to maturity, it is the return on a bond at a given price.

book value   The difference between a company's assets and liabilities.

bubble   An increase in the price of an asset for reasons other than an increase in the true value of the asset.

bull market   A term that is used to describe the stock market when stock values are rising.

call   When a borrower pays a bond off early.

capital gain   The increase in value of an asset from the time of purchase to time of sale.

capital investing   When businesses buy plant and/or equipment.

capitalization   The value of stock that is held by the public.

capital loss   The decrease in value of an asset from the time of purchase to time of sale.

certificate of deposit   An investment instrument that pays a fixed rate of interest for a specified period of time and that has penalties for early withdrawal.

common stock   Stock in a company that allows the investor to vote on matters that come before the board. When dividends are issued, the amount that common stockholders receive depends upon the profitability of the company.

compounding period   The frequency with which compounding occurs.

compound interest   Interest paid on both principal and accrued interest.

convertible bonds   Bonds that can be converted to common stock.

convertible preferred stock   Stock that is issued as preferred stock but that can be converted to common stock.

coupon payments   The periodic interest payments generated by some bonds.

credit union   A financial institution that is owned by its members.

current yield   The stated interest rate for a bond.

defined benefit plan   A retirement plan where the benefits received are guaranteed.

defined contribution plan   A retirement plan where the contributions into the plan are guaranteed, but the benefits are not.

discount bonds   Also called zero coupon bonds because they do not pay interest over the life of the bond, reducing (or discounting) their price.

diversification   The practice of spreading investments over a variety of instruments to reduce risk.

dividend   A portion of a company's profit that is paid out to stock holders.

dollar cost averaging   The practice of investing a fixed amount at regular intervals rather than trying to predict the highs and lows of the market.

Dow Jones Industrial Average   A stock index of the 30 largest corporations trading at the New York Stock Exchange.

Dutch auction   A process of selling an initial public offering directly to the public whereby investors bid on shares of stock and at the end of the auction, all the shares are sold at the lowest price.

equities   Another name for stocks, or ownership of corporations.

expected return   The return associated with a particular outcome, weighted by the probability that the outcome will occur.

face value   The amount that the borrowers agrees to pay the bond holder at the maturity date.

Federal Deposit Insurance Corporation (FDIC)   An independent agency that regulates the banking system, including providing deposit insurance.

federal funds rate   The interest rate at which Federal Reserve member banks can borrow money from each other.

Federal Reserve System   Created in 1913, it is composed of 12 regions, each with its own Federal Reserve Bank, for the purpose of regulating the money supply.

Federal Savings and Loan Insurance Corporation (FSLIC)   An independent agency that provides deposit insurance for consumers with deposits in savings and loan associations.

fixed annuity   An annuity where the investor is guaranteed a fixed rate of return.

fixed income investment   An investment, such as bonds, that provide a predictable, steady stream of returns.

general obligation bonds   Municipal bonds that have a guaranteed repayment.

growth stock   A stock which is expected to grow at least 15 percent a year.

high yield bonds   Also called junk bonds, these are bonds that are rated Ba or lower.

indexed annuity   An annuity where the return is tied to a financial index.

index fund   A stock mutual fund with a manager who does not pick individual funds, but includes the stocks that are contained in a particular index.

individual retirement account (IRA)   A privately-held retirement account that has tax deductible contributions (subject to income limits), but whose disbursements are taxable upon withdrawal.

inflation risk The risk that an investment's return will not keep pace with inflation.

initial public offering The first offering of a stock to the general public, usually made to investment banks.

insider trading Using information that is not public in order to gain from the buying and selling of investments.

interest rate risk The risk that an investment loses its value due to changes in the interest rate.

intermediate bond fund A bond fund that contains bonds that mature in four to 10 years.

investing Saving or buying instruments now in order to realize a financial gain in the future.

investment grade bonds Bonds that are rated Baa or higher.

junk bonds Bonds that are rated Ba or lower, also called high yield bonds.

large-cap company A company whose value of publicly-held stock is at least $100 million.

leverage Using borrowed money to invest, with the expectation of a larger return.

limit order An instruction from an investor to a broker that sets a maximum price the investor is willing to pay for a stock.

liquidity The ease with which an asset can be converted into cash.

load A fee that is charged when shares of a mutual fund are bought or sold.

long position Buying stock with the expectation that the stock price will rise.

long-term bond fund A bond fund that contains bonds that mature in more than 10 years.

margin The process of an investor borrowing money from a broker in order to purchase stock, using the stock as collateral for the loan.

market order An instruction from an investor to a broker to exchange a stock at whatever price is necessary.

market risk   The risk that an investment will lose its value due to fluctuations in one or more markets.

maturity date   The date at which the borrower pays the bond holder the face (or par) value of the bond.

money market account   A savings account that usually pays a slightly higher rate of interest than a passbook account, but that has higher minimum deposit requirements.

money market funds   A type of mutual fund that invests in very low risk securities with a short time horizon.

mortgage backed securities   Mortgages that are bundled together to create an investment instrument.

municipal bonds   Bonds issued by state or local governments.

mutual fund   A fund that draws money from many investors and invests in a wide array of financial instruments.

NASDAQ   A stock exchange for technology stocks that trades the largest volume of stocks in the world.

national bank   A bank that has branches in most parts of the country.

National Credit Union Share Insurance Fund (NCUSIF)   An independent agency that provides deposit insurance for consumers with deposits in credit unions.

New York Stock Exchange (NYSE)   The largest stock market in the world (in terms of stock value), only large cap stocks are traded here.

Nikkei Index   A stock index of the Tokyo Stock Exchange similar to the Dow Jones Industrial Average.

no-load fund   A mutual fund that has no charge for buying and selling shares.

opportunity cost   The next best alternative when making a decision.

overdraft fee   The fee charged by a financial institution when a checking account has insufficient funds to cover a purchase made by check or debit card.

over-the-counter market   In the bond market, the secondary market where investment banks sell their holdings of bonds to other entities.

participant-directed plan   A 401(k) plan where the investor chooses which instruments to invest in.

par value   The amount the borrowers agrees to pay the bond holder at the maturity date.

passbook savings account   A basic savings account offered by financial institutions that usually have low minimum deposits and pay a low interest rate.

preferred stock   Stock whose dividends do not vary with the profitability of the company, but that are tied to an interest rate or other stable return. Holders of preferred stock do not vote on matters that come before the board.

price fixing   Any interference with the market determination of a stock price.

price-to-book ratio   A measure of stock performance constructed by dividing a stock's price by its book value (assets minus liabilities) per share.

price-to-earnings ratio   A measure of stock performance constructed by dividing a stock's price by its earnings per share.

price-to-sales ratio   A measure of stock performance constructed by dividing a stock's price by the sales per share.

primary market   The initial sale of stocks or bonds to investment banks, it is where the issuing corporation raises the money from its offering.

privately-held company   A company that is owned by those who started the company, employees, or private investors.

prospectus   A brochure about a company that issues stocks, that contains financial and other information to help potential investors ascertain the health of the company.

retained earnings   The portion of a company's profits that are kept by the company (not paid out to investors).

return   The net gain or loss that a savings instrument or investment produces.

risk aversion   The extent to which an investor wants to avoid risk in his/her investment choices.

risk free interest rate   The interest rate on short-term bonds issued by the federal government.

risk of loss of principal The risk that the amount invested, the principal, will be lost.

Roth IRA An individual retirement account where the contributions are not tax deductible, but whose investments grow tax free and the disbursements are not taxed.

rule of 72 A quick way to compute how many years it would take for a deposit to double, it is 72 divided by the interest rate.

savings and loan association A financial institution that is often owned by its members, whose main function is to provide loans for buying homes.

secondary market The market in which investment banks sell their holdings of stocks or bonds to other entities.

Securities and Exchange Commission A federal agency that is charged with overseeing securities markets.

selling short Buying stock with the expectation that the stock price will fall.

sell stop An instruction from an investor to a broker to sell a stock if the price falls below a certain level.

short position Also called selling short, it is buying stock with the expectation that the stock price will fall.

short-term bond fund A bond fund that contains bonds that mature in less than four years.

small-cap company A corporation whose publicly-held stock value is less than $100 million.

spread The difference between an ask (selling price) and a bid (buying price).

Standard and Poor's 500 (S&P) A stock index of 500 corporations that trade on the New York Stock Exchange.

stock A portion of ownership of a corporation.

stock index A way of measuring the value of several different stocks that are similar in some way.

syndicate A group of investment banks that assist in selling the initial public offering of a company's stock.

Treasury bills The shortest-term bonds issued by the Treasury Department, they are issued in maturities of 91 days, 182 days or 364 days.

Treasury bonds   The longest-term bonds issued by the Treasury Department, usually issued with a 30-year maturity date.

Treasury notes   A medium-term bond issued by the Treasury Department, they are issued in maturities of two, three, five, and 10 years.

trustee-directed plan   A 401(k) plan where an employee of the company, the trustee, makes the decisions as to which investments are made.

underwriter   An investment bank that leads a company through the process of issuing stock.

value stock   A stock whose price is lower than normal because of a temporary, correctable problem.

variable annuity   An annuity where the investor is responsible for directing funds to various investments.

venture capitalist   Someone who invests in a new company.

yield to maturity   The return on a bond at a given bond price.

zero coupon bonds   Also called discount bonds, they do not pay interest during the life of the bond.

Answer Key

1. B
2. C
3. C
4. C
5. B
6. D
7. B
8. D
9. A
10. C
11. A
12. C

 # Bibliography

"Annuities for Dummies." Available online. URL:
http://www.freeannuityrates.com/annuities/article.
php?title=Annuities-for-Dummies. Accessed March
2011.

Coleman, Hank. "Understanding Expected Value and
Risk Tolerance for Your Investments." Available
online. URL: http://ownthedollar.com/2009/10/
understanding-expected-risk-tolerance-investments/.
Accessed March 2011.

Federal Deposit Insurance Corporation. Available online. URL: http://www.fdic.gov. Accessed March 2011.

Federal Reserve. Available online. URL: http://www.
federalreserve.gov. Accessed March 2011.

Financing Your Future. New York: Council for Economic
Education, 2007. DVD.

Investopedia. "Bond Basics: Different Types of Bonds."
Available online. URL: http://www.investopedia.com/
university/bonds/bonds4.asp. Accessed March 2011.

Morton, John S., and Mark C. Schug. *Bringing Home
the Gold: Financial Fitness for Life, Grades 9–12.* New
York: National Council on Economic Education,
2001.

TreasuryDirect. "Treasury Bonds." Available online.
URL: http://www.treasurydirect.gov/indiv/products/
prod_tbonds_glance.htm. Accessed March 2011.

U.S. Department of State. "How Stock Prices are Determined." Available online. URL: http://economics. about.com/od/stocksandmarkets/a/stock_prices.htm. Accessed March 2011.

 Index

Note: *Italic* page numbers refer to tables, charts, and illustrations.

A

actively managed funds 100–101, 115
American Stock Exchange (AMEX) 76–77, 115
annual percentage yield 28–31, 97–98, 115. *See also* compound interest
annuities 105–107, 115
ask orders 78–80, 82, 115
ATMs (automated teller machines) 16, 19–20, 21, 115
average returns *70–72*

B

banking 10–26. *See also* economy; Federal Reserve System; interest
  choosing a bank 15–24
  fees 16–18, 19–20, 24, 120
  laws and legislation 13–14, 17–18
  services provided by 14–15
  writing and tracking checks *22–24, 23*
bear market 71, 74, 89–91, 116
Berkshire Hathaway 90
beta 38, 116
bid orders 78–80, 82, 116
board of governors 11, 116
bond laddering 60–*61,* 116

bond market 42–62
  defined 42–45, 116
  economy and 47, 50, 58–*59*
  how it works 45–46
  mutual funds and 101
  prices 46–49
  ratings 56–59
  risk and return 45, 49–50, 51, 54, 55, *59*–61
  time horizon and 59–*61*
  types of bonds 43, 50–56
bond yields 47–49, 57–59, 116
book value 86, 116
bubble 94–95, 116
Buffet, Warren *90*
bull market 71, 74, 75, 116

C

call 49, 54, 116
capital gains 30–31, 72, 116
capital investing 3, 116
capitalization 74, 116
capital losses 72, 116
certificates of deposit (CDs) 25, 28–31, 34, 116
college, saving for 107–108
common stock 72–73, 116
compounding period 9–10, 117
compound interest 3–10, 27, 28–31, 102, 117
Consumer Price Index (CPI) 53

convertible bonds 54–55, 73, 117
convertible preferred stock 73, 117
corporate bonds 54–55
corporate money funds 97, 98
coupon payments 43, 46–49,
     57–58, 117
credit unions 14–15, 15–25, 117.
     See also interest
current yield 48, 117

D

defined benefit plans 101–102,
     117
defined contribution plans 102
Di Modica, Arturo 75
discount bonds 43, 117
diversification 39–41, 99–100, 117
dividends 71–72, 85, 91, 117
dollar cost averaging 40–41, 117
Dow Jones Industrial Average
     (DJIA) 76, 117
Dutch auctions 69–70, 117

E

economy
     bond market and 47, 50, 58–59
     effects of mortgage-backed
          securities on 55–56
     financial panics in history
          10–11, 93–95
     inflation 24, 33, 53, 59, 119
     interest rates and 11–13, 25–26
     stock market and 82–83, 93–95
educational savings plans 107–108
EE bonds 52–53
equities 63, 117
expected return 36–38, 118

F

face value 43, 118
Federal Deposit Insurance Corpo-
     ration (FDIC) 13–14, 96, 118

federal funds rate 11–13, 25–26,
     50, 118
Federal Home Loan Mortgage
     Corporation (Freddie Mac)
     55
Federal National Mortgage Asso-
     ciation (Fannie Mae) 55
Federal Reserve Act of 1913 10–11
Federal Reserve Bank 93, 116
Federal Reserve System 10–14, *12,*
     25–26, 50, 93, 116, 118
fees and penalties
     banking 16–18, 19–20, 24, 120
     mutual funds 100
     retirement accounts 104, 107
financial institutions. *See* banking;
     credit unions; savings and
     loan associations
financial literacy vii–ix
Fitch IBCA 56
529 plans 108, 115
fixed annuities 106, 118
fixed income investments 45, 49,
     118
401(k) plans 102–103, 115
403(b) plans 103, 115

G

Geico Insurance 90
general obligation bonds 54, 118
government. *See also* laws and
     legislation; taxes
     bonds 43, 49–54
     money market instruments 97,
          98–99, 122, 123
Government National Mortgage
     Association (Ginnie Mae) 55
Graham, Ben 90
Great Depression 93–95
growth stocks 83–85, *84,* 118

H

high yield bonds 57, 118

I

I bonds 52–53
index funds 100–101, 118
indexed annuities 107, 118
individual retirement accounts
    (IRAs) 103–105, 118
inflation 24, 33, 53, 59, 119
inflation risk 33, 119
initial public offering (IPO) 65,
    66–70, *68*, 119
insider trading 92, 95, 119
interest
    bond prices and 47, 49–50,
        52–53
    compound 3–10, 27, 28–31,
        102, 117
    compounding period 9–10,
        117
    economy and 11–13, 25–26
    federal funds rate 11–13,
        25–26, 50, 118
    Rule of 72 8–9, 122
    savings accounts and 24–25,
        28, 30–31, 34, 121
    stock market and 82–83
interest rate risk 33, 119
intermediate bond funds 101, 119
investment banks 46
investment grade bonds 57, 119
investments 3, 90, 96–109, 119.
    See also bond market; risk
    and return; stock market
    college savings 107–108
    money market funds 96–99,
        120
    mutual funds 99–101, 120
    retirement accounts 101–107

J

junk bonds 57, 119

L

large-cap companies 74, 119

laws and legislation
    banking industry 13–14, 17–18
    stock market 67, 92–93, 122
leverage 88, 119
limit orders 87, 88–89, 119
liquidity 34, 119
load funds 100, 119
London Stock Exchange 77
long *position* 91, 119
long-term bond funds 101, 119

M

margin 87–88, 93–95, 119
market orders 78, 87, 88, 119
market risk 33, 120. *See also* risk
    and return
maturity date 43, 120
money market accounts 25, 28,
    30–31, 34, 120
    money market funds v. 96
money market funds (MMFS)
    96–99, 120
Moody's Investors Services 56–57
mortgage-backed securities
    55–56, 120
mortgage banks (savings and
    loans) 14, 122
municipal bonds 53–54, 120
mutual funds 99–101, 120

N

National Association of Securities
    Dealers Automated Quota-
    tions (NASDAQ) 76, 120
national banks 11, 120
National Credit Union Share
    Insurance Fund (NCUSIF)
    14, 120
New York Stock Exchange (NYSE)
    65–66, 74–77, *79*, 120
Nikkei Index 77, 83, 120
no-load funds 100, 120

O

Obama, Barack *90*
online banking 21
opportunity cost 1, 38, 120
opting in 17–18
overdraft fees 16–18, 19–20, 24, 120
over-the-counter-markets (OTCs) 46, 120

P

participated-directed plans 103, 121
par value 43, 121
passbook savings accounts 24–25, 28, 30–31, 34, 121
penalties. *See* fees and penalties
preferred stock 72–73, 121
prepaid plans 108
price fixing 92–93, 121
price-to-book ratio 86, 121
price-to-earnings ratio 85–86, 91, 121
price-to-sales ratio 86, 121
primary market 46, 68, 72, 121
privately-held companies 64–65, 121
prospectus 67, 121

R

recession 94–95
retained earnings 71, 121
retirement accounts 101–107
return on investment 27–31, 121
risk and return 27–41
    bond market and 45, 49–50, 51, 54, 55, 59–61
    calculating 28–31, 35–38
    diversification 39–41, 99–100, 117
    managing 39–41
    money market funds 97–99
    stock market *70–72, 83–85, 84*

tolerance *35–41*
    types of risk 32–35
risk aversion 38, 121
risk free interest rate 49–50, 51, 121
risk of loss of principal 32–33, 122
risk/reward pyramid *35–41*
risk tolerance *35–41*
"road show" 67
Roth IRAs 104, 122
Rule of 72 *8–9*, 53, 122

S

savings 1–3, *2*, 29, 107–108. *See also* return on investment; risk and return
savings accounts (passbook) 24–25, 28, 30–31, 34, 121
savings and loan associations 14, 122
savings bonds 52–53
secondary market 46, 68, 72, 122
Securities and Exchange Commission (SEC) 67, 92–93, 122
sell stops 89, 122
selling short 89–90, 122
short position 89–90, 122
short-term bond funds 101, 122
small-cap companies 76, 122
speculation 94–95
spread 78, 122
Standard and Poor's 56
Standard and Poor's 500 (S&P) 76, 122
stock index 76, 122
stock market 63–95
    analysts' reports 81–82
    benefits of stocks 70–72
    buying and selling 73–77, 86–91
    choosing stocks 83–85
    crashes 93–95
    defined 63–65, 122
    economy and 82–83, 93–95

exchanges 73–77
factors affecting prices 77–85
history of 65–66, 93–95
insider trading 92, 95, 119
interest and 82–83
measuring performance 85–86
price fixing 92–93, 121
reading the stock page 91
regulation of 62, 92–93, 122
risk and return *70*–72, 83–85,
    84
stock creation 66–70
types of stocks 72–73
stockbrokers 74
syndicate 67, 122

T
taxes
    government bonds and 51,
        53, 54
    money market funds and
        98–99
    retirement accounts 102–103,
        104, *105,* 106
time horizon *59*–61. *See also* com-
    pounding period
Tokyo Stock Exchange 77

trade-offs 34–38
Treasury bills 51, 99, 122
Treasury bonds 51–53, 123
Treasury notes 51, 123
trustee-directed plans 103, 123

U
underwriters 67–70, 123

V
value stocks *84*–85, 123
variable annuities 106–107, 123
venture capitalist 65, 123

W
Wall Street *75. See also* New York
    Stock Exchange (NYSE)

Y
yield. *See* annual percentage yield
yield to maturity 48–49, 123

Z
zero coupon bonds 43, *44*–45,
    46–49, 53, 55, 123